The Perfect Storm: The Realities of Xenophobia in Contemporary South Africa

Series Editor:
Prof. Jonathan Crush

Southern African Migration Project
2008

Editorial Note

We take no satisfaction in the fact that SAMP's 50th Migration Policy Paper Series is on the subject of xenophobia in contemporary South Africa. Most of SAMP's recent work has focused on the positive relationships between migration and development. Policies to promote development-oriented migration are, however, difficult to imagine, promote and implement in an atmosphere of intolerance and anti-immigrant sentiment. We trust that the research presented in this report will bring fresh perspectives on the reasons for the xenophobic mayhem of May 2008 and workable suggestions on how to prevent a repetition. The questionnaire on which the report is based was designed by a working group consisting of Jonathan Crush (SAMP), David A. McDonald (MSP), Vincent Williams and Kate Lefko-Everett (Idasa and SAMP), David Dorey (SAMP) and Don Taylor and Roxanne la Sablonniere (McGill). These individuals are also the collective authors of this report. The fieldwork was carried out in 2006 in collaboration with Citizen Surveys. The research was financed by SAMP using funds from DFID-UK. Crush, McDonald and Taylor also wish to thank the SSHRC for support of their project on The Politics of Xenophobia in South Africa. This paper and the opinions expressed herein are those of the authors alone. We wish to thank Ashley Hill for her assistance with the report and all those who consented to interviews and gave freely of their time and attitudes.

Published by Idasa, 6 Spin Street, Church Square, Cape Town, 8001, and Southern African Research Centre, Queen's University, Canada.

Copyright Southern African Migration Project (SAMP) 2008
ISBN 978-1-920118-71-6

First published 2008
Design by Bronwen Müller
Typeset in Goudy

CONTENTS   PAGE

TABLES   PAGE

FIGURES   PAGE

EXECUTIVE SUMMARY

The world recently watched with dismay as South African citizens violently attacked foreign nationals in communities across the country. Tens of thousands of migrants were displaced, amid mass looting and destruction of foreign-owned homes, property and businesses. Senior officials and politicians seemed bemused and perplexed by the xenophobic violence. The media was quick to advance several theories about the mayhem. One focused on historical factors, particularly South Africa's divisive and alienating apartheid past. Another blamed poverty and the daily struggle for existence in many of South Africa's poorer communities. A third criticized the ANC government for poor service delivery and a failure to redistribute the fruits of the post-apartheid economic boom to the poor. Finally, the country's immigration policies were seen as at fault. None of these theories explicitly tackles the phenomenon of xenophobia itself.

In late 2006 SAMP undertook a national survey of the attitudes of the South African population towards foreign nationals in the country. The data from this survey allows us to analyze the state of the nation's mind on immigration, immigrants and refugees in the period immediately prior to the recent upsurge of xenophobic violence in South Africa. By comparing the results with those of previous surveys conducted by SAMP in the 1990s, we are also able to see if attitudes have changed and in what ways. Are they better now than they were in the days that prompted the South African Human Rights Commission to set up its Roll Back Xenophobia Campaign and partner with SAMP in a study of immigration, xenophobia and human rights in the country? Has xenophobia softened or hardened in the intervening years? Are xenophobic attitudes as widespread and vitriolic as they were then? How many South Africans were poised, in 2006, to turn their negative thoughts about foreign nationals into actions to "cleanse" their neighbourhoods and streets of fellow Africans?

The 2006 SAMP Xenophobia Survey shows that South Africa exhibits levels of intolerance and hostility to outsiders unlike virtually anything seen in other parts of the world. For example:

- Compared to citizens of other countries worldwide, South Africans are the least open to outsiders and want the greatest restrictions on immigration. Earlier data showed a hardening of attitudes in the late 1990s. The proportion of people wanting strict limits or a total prohibition on immigration rose from 65% in 1997 to 78% in 1999 and the proportion of those favouring immigration if there were jobs available fell from 29% to 12%.
- Similarly restrictive views still prevail. Two changes were evident in 2006, one positive and one negative. On the positive side,

the proportion who agree to employed-related immigration rose from 12% in 1999 to 23% in 2006. In part, this reflects the immigration policy shift in 2002 which promoted a new skills-based approach. On the negative, the proportion of those wanting a total ban on immigration increased from 25% in 1999 to 35% in 2006. And 84% feel that South Africa is allowing "too many" foreign nationals into the country.

- Nearly 50% support or strongly support the deportation of foreign nationals including those living legally in South Africa. Only 18% strongly oppose such a policy.
- Nearly three-quarters (74%) support a policy of deporting anyone who is not contributing economically to South Africa.
- Some 61% support the deportation of foreign nationals who test positive for HIV or have AIDS with a mere 9% strongly opposed.
- If migrants are allowed in, South Africans want them to come alone, as they were forced to in the apartheid period. Less than 20% think it should be easier for families of migrants to come with them to South Africa.
- Nearly three-quarters (72%) think that foreign nationals should carry personal identification with them at all times (the same as in 1999). Only 4% strongly opposed the suggestion.
- The proportion of South Africans wanting their borders to be electrified increased from 66% in 1999 to 76% in 2006. Only 2% are strongly opposed to such a policy.
- South Africans do not want it to be easier for foreign nationals to trade informally with South Africa (59% opposed), to start small businesses in South Africa (61% opposed) or to obtain South African citizenship (68% opposed).

Many post-apartheid migrants to South Africa are asylum-seekers and refugees. How do South Africans view the issue of refugee protection and South Africa's responsibilities towards them? The Survey found that:

- South Africans are divided on refugee protection with 47% supporting protection and 30% opposed. Nearly 20% have no opinion on the matter.
- Nearly three quarters are opposed to increasing the number of refugees currently in the country.
- Two-thirds are against offering permanent residence to refugees who have been in the country for more than 5 years.
- As many as half favour a policy of requiring all refugees to live in border camps. Only 6% are strongly opposed.
- Only 30% agree with allowing refugees to work.
- And 60% want a policy of mandatory HIV testing of refugees.

In the 1990s, SAMP found that many South Africans were generally not in favour of extending basic constitutional rights to foreign nationals (to which they are legally entitled). In 1999, less than 20% felt that refugees should always be entitled to legal and police protection. In the case of "illegal immigrants" the figure was less than 10%. Temporary workers and visitors were viewed a little more sympathetically although only 13% felt they should automatically enjoy police protection.

There have been some changes for the better since 1999. In 2006, there were drops in the proportion of South Africans who would deny basic rights to refugees and temporary workers and visitors. But the majority of South Africans still do not believe that either should automatically enjoy police or legal protection.

Since so many South Africans also believe that the majority of foreign nationals in their country are here illegally, this means, in effect, that they believe that basic rights should be denied to many if not most foreign nationals. With the exception of treatment for AIDS, at least two-thirds of South Africans still feel that irregular migrants in the country should be extended no rights or protections. Given that the police are believed to be major beneficiaries of the presence of irregular migrants (through bribery and protection rackets), this is alarming indeed.

While South Africans clearly favour highly restrictive immigration policies, it does not necessarily follow that they dislike foreign nationals per se (which would make them xenophobic as opposed to merely defensive and protectionist). In South Africa, however, the 2006 Xenophobia Survey shows that negative opinions on immigration policy go hand-in-hand with hostile attitudes towards foreign nationals. If xenophobes view foreign nationals as a threat, they will generally attribute negative motives to "the invader." In 1999, 48% of South Africans saw migrants from neighbouring countries as a "criminal threat", some 37% said they were a threat to jobs and the economy, and 29% that they brought disease. Only 24% said there was nothing to fear.

South Africans continue to consider foreign nationals a threat to the social and economic well-being of their country. Indeed, along certain indicators, attitudes have hardened since 1999. The proportion arguing that foreign nationals use up resources grew by 8% from 59% in 1999 to 67% in 2006. The association of migrants with crime also intensified (45% in 1999 to 67% in 2006) as did the idea that migrants bring disease (24% in 1999 to 49% in 2006). The only positive sign was that more South Africans (6% more) felt that foreign nationals bring needed skills to South Africa. At the same time, two-thirds still believe that they are not needed.

Foreign nationals are often seen in South Africa as "job-stealers." South Africans are also sometimes accused of treating all foreign nationals as an undifferentiated group. The Survey therefore tried to assess whether South Africans distinguish between migrants in terms of where they are from. On these issues the Survey found the following:

- Migrants from North America and Europe are regarded more favourably than those from other SADC countries who, in turn, are more favourably perceived than those from the rest of Africa. However, these preferences are purely relative. A majority of South Africans have an unfavourable impression of migrants wherever they are from.
- Within Africa, migrants from Botswana, Lesotho and Swaziland are regarded in the most favourable light. Thirty-nine percent of those surveyed, for example, hold a favourable view of Basotho. Mozambicans (who only 14% of South African view favourably) and Zimbabweans (12%) are viewed much less favourably. Most unpopular of all are Angolans, Somalis and Nigerians.
- The supposed "economic threat" posed by immigrants does not appear to be based on personal experience as very few respondents have experience of losing a job to a foreign national (85%). Around two-thirds say they do not know anyone who has personally lost a job or heard of anyone in their community who has.
- In SAMP surveys in the 1990s, respondents were asked how much contact they had with people from neighbouring countries in Southern Africa (from which the vast majority of migrants come). Surprisingly few was the answer (80% had little or no contact in 1997 and 60% in 1999). In the 1999 SAMP survey only 4% of respondents said they had "a great deal of contact." SAMP concluded that the vast majority of South Africans form their attitudes in a vacuum, relying mainly on hearsay and media and other representations.
- In 2006, the proportion with little or no contact had hardly changed. What has changed is the proportion with no contact at all (down from 60% in 1997 to 32% in 2006) and with a great deal of contact (up from 4% in 1997 to 17% in 2006). In other words, the majority of attitudes are still formed independent of personal interaction with migrants. However, more South Africans are interacting with non-nationals (and presumably having their prejudices confirmed by such interaction).

In 1999, SAMP was unable to identify a "typical" profile of a xenophobic person. Strong negative attitudes seemed to be held irrespective of race, gender, education, socio-economic status or any other variable. For the 2006 survey, SAMP developed a composite "xenophobia" score for each individual ranging from 0 (very xenophobic) to 10 (not xenophobic at all). These scores were then grouped by variables such as race, class, income and so on. The following emerged:

- On the scale of zero to ten, the average score was 3.95, suggesting that, in general, levels of xenophobia are high. There were differences between race groups, however. Coloured respondents have the highest levels of xenophobia. Whites are more xenophobic than blacks and Asians/Indians are least xenophobic.
- Respondents with Afrikaans as their home language display much higher levels of xenophobia than all other language groups. Next were Xhosa-speakers followed by Sotho-speakers, Zulu-speakers, English-speakers and Tsonga/Shangaan-speakers.
- Differences can also be seen by class. Here we see a bimodal distribution with respondents who described themselves as "upper class" equally as xenophobic as those from the "lower class." Both are slightly more xenophobic than respondents in other class groups including the "working class." The "middle class" is least xenophobic.
- In terms of income categories, average xenophobia scores were highest in the lowest income categories and generally declined with increasing income. Those in the R8,000 to R8,999 per month and R18,000 – R19,999 per month categories showed slightly higher levels than predicted. In other words there is a strong correlation between xenophobia and income but it is not absolute with some wealthier groups displaying higher levels of xenophobia.
- On average, xenophobic attitudes appear to be more prevalent among those with less education. Xenophobia scores were greatest amongst the respondents who had no formal schooling and decreased in intensity with progressively higher levels of education.
- Levels of xenophobia differ slightly by employment status. The unemployed and those looking for work have slightly higher levels of xenophobia than the employed. However, the difference of greatest statistical significance was between those who were employed full time and pensioners, who displayed the most xenophobic attitudes of any group.
- Political party affiliation also shows slight differences. Democratic Alliance (DA) supporters have slightly higher levels of xenophobia than ANC supporters.

In general, xenophobic attitudes are stronger amongst whites than blacks and stronger amongst the poor and working class and the wealthy than the middle class.

The Survey then asked South Africans what, if anything, they would do about foreign nationals living in their communities. First, they were asked about the likelihood of taking part in actions to prevent people from other Southern African countries from moving into their neighbour-hood, operating a business in the area, being in the same classroom as their children and becoming a co-worker. In both 1999 and 2006 almost the same proportion (around a third) said it was likely or very likely that they would take action.

A related question asked what sorts of action they would take against foreign nationals. Most said they would confine themselves to "snitch-ing" to the police (44%), community associations (36%) and employers (32%). Some 16% of South Africans said they were prepared to combine with others to force foreign nationals to leave the area and 9% would use violence in the process. This surely indicates that the violence of May 2008 could well have been even more widespread or may become so in the near future. At the very least, it suggests that a sizeable minority approves of the actions of others.

An overview of xenophobia in South Africa since the democratic elections in 1994 shows that the "perfect storm" of May 2008 did not spring out of nowhere. The rise of xenophobia in the 1990s cannot be isolated from the country's apartheid past of racial and class division and animosity, racist immigration policies, a siege mentality and attitudes of uniqueness and superiority towards the rest of Africa. Equally it cannot be divorced from new migration streams, legal and irregular, to post-1990 South Africa. But rather than seek ways to deal with, accommodate and integrate the new African migrants, South Africans began to rail against them, to blame them for everything from crime to HIV/AIDS to unem-ployment, and to deport them in their hundreds of thousands. Only a handful of South Africans were ever prosecuted for employing people illegally. A culture of corruption infested dealings between the state and foreign nationals. Police and immigration officials found rich pickings in the pockets of desperate migrants.

Facilitated by a decade of in-fighting on immigration policy, irresponsi-ble political statements and an uncritical and xenophobic press, the can-cer spread. At first, with some exceptions, it remained in the heads and words of South Africans. But when thought turned to action, xenophobic thugs discovered that they could act with virtual impunity. Increasingly their "cause" became less random and took on the character (and even-tual horror) of "ethnic cleansing" campaigns in other parts of the world.

In 2002, a new Immigration Act promised action and a systematic rooting out of xenophobia in the public service and society at large. In practice, some isolated anti-xenophobia measures were taken within the Department of Home Affairs to educate officials. But the South African Human Rights Commission wound up its Roll Back Xenophobia campaign and when SAMP published two reports on xenophobia in the media these were ignored (unlike its policy research on other issues such as the brain drain.) The uncomfortable fact of xenophobia sunk from view in the public policy domain. And when xenophobic violence began to escalate in 2006, there were ritual condemnations and some prosecutions but not much else.

This report therefore concludes that there has been both a political and a moral failure. Morally, South Africans have let themselves down by tending and nurturing xenophobia while engaging in rounds of hearty self-congratulation about their constitution, their deep respect for human rights and their leadership role in Africa and the world. In other words, as the 2006 Survey confirmed, xenophobia and hostility to (particularly) other Africans is not the preserve of a lunatic fringe but represents the convictions of the majority of citizens. When one journalist wrote recently that "we are all guilty", he was speaking truth to power.

Some ANC politicians have questioned how South Africans could attack black Africans from countries that had been so accommodating to South African exiles in the days of the anti-apartheid struggle. The key question is whether the exile experience has any resonance or meaning for the general populace. If everyone believed that South Africans should treat other Africans with tolerance and acceptance as pay-back for their past support, this should be reflected in positive attitudes towards the role played by those countries in the past and the way they treated exiled South Africans. Respondents in the Survey were therefore asked how well they thought South African exiles had been treated in other African countries. Nearly 20% of the respondents felt that the exiles had been treated badly. Another 41% had no opinion one way or the other. Only 39 percent agreed that they had been treated well or very well. In other words, it might be argued that nearly two out of three South Africans find the idea of reciprocity for past support of the liberation struggle either wrong or irrelevant. Further questioning would be necessary to prove this hypothesis.

A section of the media spent much of May 2008 criticizing the ANC government for the xenophobic mayhem, for failing to "deliver," for intensified poverty and inequality, for corruption and ineptitude. Quite naturally, government denied responsibility with a catalogue of its post-apartheid successes. This paper argues that this debate misses a fundamental point. Xenophobia is a destructive and reactionary force wherever it is found – in France, in Indonesia, in India, in South Africa. In a world of nation-states where national sovereignty is paramount, there is potential for it to rear its head in any migrant-receiving country. The onus is therefore on the receiving state to design, implement and actively pursue policies and programmes at all levels of society aimed at fostering tolerance, diversity, multi-culturalism and regional and global citizenship. In South Africa, government spending on anti-xenophobia education has

7

been minimal. Hard-pressed NGOs and refugee groups do their best but cannot draw on the resources available to the state. Public education that reaches deep into the schools, into communities and into state institutions is essential. So too is strong political will and leadership which is action-oriented not just rhetorical.

This report has argued that further xenophobic violence, even a repetition of May 2008, is almost inevitable without the implementation of short and longer-term measures. Civil society, community structures and NGOs have a critical role to play. Our concern is with the state and with what policy measures should be recommended. We make the following recommendations here:

- All past and future perpetrators of xenophobic violence should be vigorously prosecuted. There are signs that this is indeed what the state intends though the penalties should be harsh and exacting for all of those who broke the law, destroyed and stole property and engaged in rape and murder. This is necessary not only to make an example of xenophobic thuggery but to dissuade similar actions in the future. The citizenry needs to know that despite its own dislike of foreigners, taking the law into its own hands will not be tolerated. The state also needs to revisit past incidents of xenophobic violence and prosecute those involved as well.

- Too many South Africans, and too many police and officials, have engaged for far too long in exploiting the vulnerability of foreign nationals. Corruption in all aspects of the immigration system needs to become more costly than it is worth to the perpetrators. At the same time, South African employers who flaunt labour laws in their hiring and employment of migrants need to be exposed and prosecuted.

- The deeper problem of widespread and entrenched xenophobic attitudes needs to be seriously addressed. There is no reason why the majority of citizens should favour a particular immigration policy provided they are well-informed about the purpose, nature and impacts of that policy. But there is absolutely no reason, or excuse, for that to be accompanied by abuse, hatred and hostility towards migrants and "fellow" Africans in particular. Attitudes that are so entrenched, pervasive and negative need to be attacked with the same commitment that state and civil society has shown towards the scourge of racism in post-apartheid South Africa.

- South Africa urgently needs an antidote to a decade of political inaction on xenophobia. Since 1994, South African attitudes have only hardened. What has been done is too little, much too late. Required now is a broad, high-profile, multi-media, government-initiated and sponsored anti-xenophobia education program that reaches into schools, workplaces, communities and the corridors of the public service. This program should be systematic and ongoing. The programme needs to breed tolerance, celebration of diversity and the benefits of interaction with peoples from other countries.

- South Africans need to be educated about immigration and the benefits of managed migration. They need to know that immigration is not really as harmful as they think. They need to understand that immigration can be extremely beneficial. They need to know if it is. They need to be disabused of the myths and stereotypes they hold dear. They need to know what rights foreign nationals are entitled to when in South Africa. They need to be African and world leaders in refugee rights protection. They need to understand that South Africa is a member of a region and a world and has responsibilities to both. There needs to be informed public debate and discussion about pan-Africanism, the economic benefits of South Africa's interaction with Africa, and the need for immigrants. They need to abandon a myopic nationalistic siege mentality.

- The events of May 2008 may provide the necessary spur to political action. Certainly the humanitarian response of many in civil society suggests that there are South Africans who are repulsed and ashamed by what their fellow citizens have done. Officials and politicians also need to move beyond rhetoric to action and example. Strong political leadership and will is required. South Africa cannot hold its head up in Africa, in SADC, at the African Union, at any other international forum, if it continues to allow xenophobia to flourish. President Mbeki reacted with "disgust" to the events of May 2008. Disgust at xenophobic actions should translate into disgust at pre-existing and enabling xenophobic attitudes and a serious campaign to clear the minds of all citizens.

- With the exception of the tabloid press, the media response to May 2008 has generally fostered informed analysis and debate. It has not always been this way. The real tragedy of the last ten years is the way in which the media has mishandled the issue of xenophobia. Several research studies have shown how the media has uncritically reproduced xenophobic language and statements, time and again. The media has certainly been complicit in encouraging xenophobic attitudes among the population. They would not uncritically report the opinions of every racist they come across. No more should they uncritically tolerate the opinions of xenophobes.

- South Africa has not yet ratified the UN Convention on the Rights of All Migrant Workers and Members of their Families. The Convention is not inconsistent with South Africa's human rights and labour law. However, there has been little public debate about the treaty and knowledge of its content and implications is extremely low in official circles. South Africa should take the African lead in ratifying this convention and making the reasons clear to its own citizens. Commitment to and adherence to the Convention would help to clarify for all exactly what rights and entitlements foreign nationals have when in South Africa.

- South Africa urgently needs an immigration policy overhaul. The fraught and protracted political process leading to a new Immigration Act in 2002 delivered a policy framework that is incoherent and, in many respects, unimplemented and unimplementable. Neither the post 2002 skills-based immigration policy associated with JIPSA, nor the enforcement measures contemplated by the Act, are working, precisely as SAMP and many other independent commentators predicted at the time. There is a need to develop a coherent and workable development-oriented immigration plan and to "sell" that plan to an electorate steeped in isolationism and hostility to immigration, despite the many demonstrable benefits it brings the country. No pro-active immigration plan can survive for long with a citizenry that is so uneducated about, and sceptical of, the benefits of immigration.

INTRODUCTION

> "I use perfect in the metereological sense: a storm that could
> not possibly have been worse" (Sebastian Junger 1997)

In May 2008, the rest of the world reacted with dismay, outrage and disgust as South African citizens violently attacked foreign nationals in communities across the country. Tens of thousands of migrants were displaced, amid mass looting and destruction of foreign-owned homes, property and businesses. Media coverage documented the killing of more than 60 migrants, "necklacing" and burning, widespread and vicious assaults, and allegations of rape. On Monday, 26 May, Safety and Security Minister Charles Nqakula reported that 1,384 suspects had been arrested, 342 shops looted and 213 burnt down.[1]

Statements from senior officials and politicians suggest that they were – to put it mildly – bemused and perplexed by the outbreak of xenophobic violence. In a media briefing on 20 May 2008, for example, Deputy Minister of Foreign Affairs Aziz Pahad described the "unprecedented savage attacks against South Africans and fellow Africans" as a "totally unexpected phenomenon in our country."[2] Government, Pahad stated, was "not taken by surprise by the possibility of these attacks" but rather by the "extent and nature including the violence of what we have witnessed." Pahad lamented: "You would not have thought that 14 years into our democracy we would suddenly experience such an explosion of attacks against foreigners when we have been trying through education and political processes to inform people about our vision of one Africa and an integrated Africa."[3] Deputy President Phumzile Mlambo-Ngcuka expressed similar confusion and consternation in a statement made on May 23, as widespread violence escalated in the Western Cape: "I just cannot believe that normal South Africans are anti their African brothers and sisters. I just cannot believe this."[4]

Defending government's allegedly tardy response to the first xenophobic attacks, Safety and Security Minister Charles Nqakula also described the violence as "strange", given that many South Africans had sought refuge in neighbouring countries under apartheid.[5] Also perplexed was the Minister for Home Affairs Nosiviwe Mapisa-Nqakula, whose Ministry has the most interaction with foreign nationals and who has promoted anti-xenophobia training amongst officials in her employ. At a briefing to the Parliamentary Portfolio Committee on Home Affairs on the 13 May 2008, Mapisa-Nqakula reportedly commented that it was "strange that people who had lived together for many years were suddenly at each other's throats." She speculated about the possibility of a "third force" involved in orchestrating xenophobic violence, suggesting that "there could be people who are stoking fires because these are people who

11

have been living side by side for a very long time."[6] Days later, in a radio interview on SAFM, the Minister reiterated that she was "shocked" and "puzzled" that the spate of xenophobic violence had reached such a fever pitch.

The response of the Intelligence Community was similar. NIA Director General, Manala Manzini, in what must rank as one of the stranger reactions to the situation, reportedly argued on 22 May 2008 that the violence was orchestrated "by internal and external racist elements bent on destabilising next year's general election."[7] On 23 May 2008, Minister Ronnie Kasrils reportedly admitted "that the government had been taken by surprise by the attacks." Kasrils conceded that "Of course we were aware something was brewing. It is one thing to know there is a social problem and another thing to know when that outburst will occur."[8] The sum of these government statements appears to be, at most, an awareness of xenophobia as an abstract "social problem" – to use Kasril's words – but an apparent disconnect with the possibility that violence was a possible or even likely outcome.

In stark contrast to the puzzled response of politicians, media commentators were quick to advance various theories to explain the mayhem. On 23 May 2008, the Sowetan, for example, claimed that "some rotten apples are committing inexplicable atrocities."[9] In other words, responsibility lay with a small group of sociopaths whose irrational behaviour defied explanation. At the other end of the spectrum, Andile Mngxitama suggested in City Press on 17 May 2008 that "all of South Africa is guilty."[10]

Generally, the media identified four inter-linked culprits: one historical, one material, one political and one managerial. In terms of the historical causes, Mngxitama, for example, located them "deep in our colonial and apartheid history."[11] Janet Smith, too, wrote of South African's long history of hatred of otherness."[12] While the precise connections between " history" and the present crisis were not articulated by either, these journalists touched on an important point: xenophobia in South Africa has a past which we ignore at our peril.

Those preferring material explanations for the violence cited a massive income gap and "gnawing poverty" as the cause of growing xenophobia.[13] Typical was the editorial in the Mail & Guardian of 2 June 2006:

> Frustrated by escalating costs of living and competition for houses and jobs, poor South Africans, mostly uneducated about the role that fellow Africans played in the South African liberation struggle, are picking the easiest scapegoats amongst them – foreigners.[14]

Here, not only is historical amnesia seen as a direct cause of the attacks, but poverty is the driving force behind them. Certainly, the incidence of xenophobic violence is strongly correlated with the geography of poverty. But this simply begs the question of why not all poor areas (in many of which foreign nationals are resident) erupted or why poor South Africans aren't attacking each other with similar ferocity. Academic commentators have similarly tended to target poverty and inequality as major precipitating factors.[15]

Phumza Macanda blamed the "failure to spread South Africa's economic gains to the poor" claiming that this has "fuelled violence against immigrants and could spark wider unrest."[16] Whose failure? Implicit here is a veiled criticism of the state. Journalists like Macanda posit a political or, more accurately, a politicised explanation for the violence. They ask who is responsible for the poverty and inequality that "causes" xenophobia and identify government and the ANC. So while politicians expressed bewilderment, journalists blamed the politicians. For example, Justice Malala writing in the Sunday Times on 19 May 2008, cited a "cocktail" mixed by the ANC: "stubborn denialism on Zimbabwe, an increasingly incompetent and corrupt police service, poor service delivery and corruption in public departments."[17] For S'Thembiso Msoni, the violence exposed the extent to which "the country's political leadership is disconnected from poor communities."[18] South Africans are frustrated with the slow pace of delivery and the lack of job opportunities.[19] Mbeki himself was accused of failing to sell pan-Africanism to his own people, so government not only apparently caused the disease, it failed to supply the antidote.[20]

The theme of government culpability was taken up by other commentators. Saki Macozoma, President of Business Leadership South Africa, saw the events as the result of "pent-up frustration over poor service delivery, lack of leadership and the legacy of apartheid" combining with "a culture of violence and general criminality" to produce conditions for the "perfect storm."[21] At the other end of the spectrum, Blade Nzimande of the South African Communist Party, blamed the political failures of the ANC, seeing the violence as "one expression of the weakening and near decay of the structure of the ANC on the ground and their inability to lead progressive community struggles and failures to detect resulting plans against our African brothers and sisters."[22] Unsurprisingly, government quickly denied any connections between its policies and the violence.[23]

The themes of poverty, inequality and government failure were enthusiastically embraced by the foreign media. The New York Times, for example, claimed that xenophobia had escalated from an occasional malady to a contagion. The root cause was the gap between rich and poor and disillusionment by South Africans "at the bottom."[24] The Times of London argued that Mbeki had "failed spectacularly" to channel the proceeds of a post-apartheid economic boom to the poor in the townships and to deal firmly with Zimbabwe (the source of a growing number of desperate and destitute migrants).[25] Canadian correspondent for the Toronto Globe and Mail, Stephanie Nolen, argued that "the culture of xenophobia originates at the top: the notorious Department of Home Affairs treats refugees and asylum seekers abysmally. Multiple reports from human-rights organizations have documented how corrupt officials demand bribes to extend asylum papers and police officers tear up valid papers, then deport 'illegals.'"[26]

Finally, some commentators relate the xenophobic violence to the failure by the state to control the country's borders. The IFP, for example, argues that xenophobia is a result of the ANC leaving South Africa's borders "wide open."[27] South Africa, the general argument goes, is being "flooded" by Africa's poor and destitute. During the 1990s, outsiders were described as "aliens." Since 2002, they have become "foreigners." Supposedly more neutral, this phrase has the same intent: to clearly differentiate those who "belong" from those who do not. Descriptions of the in-migration of aliens or foreigners are usually accompanied by vacuous "estimates" of the numbers involved, invariably in the "millions." Xenophobia, in this specious view, is an inevitable consequence of a failure by the state to control migration.

The logical extension of this argument was recently articulated by the Human Sciences Research Council (HSRC) as follows: "It is essential that government move urgently and effectively to protect South Africa's borders and points-of-entry. No migration policy or strategy aimed at alleviating xenophobic tensions can be contemplated if the national borders are porous and people can come and go as they please."[28] In other words, keep "aliens" and "foreigners" out and there will be no xenophobia. What this fails to recognize, of course, is that this is precisely what the South African state has been trying to do since 1994, actually since 1910, without much success. The post-apartheid state could no more seal its borders than the apartheid state before it. And why should it when cross-border movement is a longstanding historical reality, when freer movement is inevitable as regional integration proceeds and when managed migration brings many (unacknowledged) benefits to South Africa?

Influential commentator on international affairs, Gwynne Dwyer, completely missed the mark when he identified the "root problem" as government's "non-interventionist" and "open doors" policy on immigration and its "refusal to control or even count the number of people arriving in South Africa from other African countries."[29] Apparently this policy has led to "five million" illegal immigrants in South Africa. Dwyer's comments reveal a startling ignorance about migration policy in South

Africa and are of interest only so far as they reproduce the xenophobic imagery and stereotypes that are fuelling anti-immigrant violence.

None of these media commentators remotely explain how the country arrived at this pass, fourteen years into democracy, and with perhaps the most liberal and human-rights based Constitution in the world. SAMP research suggests that the current xenophobic violence is the outcome of widespread and long-standing anti-foreign sentiment and a different kind of political failure: a failure to heed the warning signs that stretch back at least a decade. There has been a growing tendency within government to view the events of May 2008 as criminal rather than xenophobic. In a recent parliamentary debate one MP proposed that the use of derogatory terms such as "makwerekwere" to describe foreign nationals be banned. Thabo Mbeki's reported response was very revealing: "the use of the term dated back many decades and could therefore not be blamed for the violence."[30] In other words, it appears that xenophobic language is acceptable and not a relevant factor.

In contrast, this report argues that xenophobic language and actions are as unacceptable and unconstitutional as racist language and actions. Xenophobic attitudes are widespread and entrenched in South Africa and not the preserve of a small (criminal) minority. Our intention is to foreground xenophobia itself as a key explanation for the xenophobic violence of May 2006. We provide an analysis of the extent and nature of xenophobia in contemporary South Africa, and give that analysis some historical depth. Fourteen years into the new dispensation, long after the first flush of nationhood has faded, are South Africans still as xenophobic as they demonstrably were in the 1990s? The report addresses the following questions:

- What is the nature of xenophobia in South Africa? A common dictionary definition of xenophobia is, quite literally, the "hatred or fear of foreigners or strangers", combining the Greek xenos (foreign) with phobos (fear). How has xenophobia infected attitudes, perceptions and, increasingly, actions towards non-nationals living in South Africa?
- Is the current violence a function of xenophobic sentiment and action or of material deprivation and political failure or both? What is striking about the response of politicians and the media to the current crisis is a failure to contextualize the roots of xenophobia in South Africa and a failure to offer any plausible explanation of the phenomenon itself. In other words, are South Africans actually xenophobic? Or, since it would be unfair and inaccurate to tar all with the same brush, which South Africans are xenophobic and why?
- What clues to the current mayhem in South Africa are there in

the current attitudes and perceptions of South Africans towards non-nationals?
- What are the policy implications for anti-xenophobia action and education in South Africa?

The report is based on the results of a 2006 national survey of South African attitudes to migration, migrants and refugees. Conducted on the eve of the "perfect storm" the survey provides important insights into the contemporary mindset of all South Africans and explains why the population was primed for just this sort of eventuality. While SAMP has been advising of the dangers of unchecked xenophobia for many years, its decision to revisit the issue of South African attitudes to migration turns out to be of much greater relevance than anticipated.

A SHORT HISTORY OF POST-APARTHEID XENOPHOBIA

In 1995, a report by the Southern African Bishops' Conference concluded: "There is no doubt that there is a very high level of xenophobia in our country .... One of the main problems is that a variety of people have been lumped together under the title of 'illegal immigrants', and the whole situation of demonising immigrants is feeding the xenophobia phenomenon." In 1996, Jonathan Crush identified a "blunt, and increasingly bellicose, mythology targeted at non-South Africans living in the country" and its use by politicians and the press to "whip up" anti-immigrant sentiment.[31] A year later, a study from the Human Sciences Research Council (HSRC) reported widespread negative attitudes to migrants among South Africans with whites the most negative.

Writing in 1998, Sheena Duncan of the Black Sash warned that the "xenophobia that is growing so quickly among South Africans is cause for serious concern." Duncan blamed politicians, bureaucrats and the media for exacerbating the situation: "They repeatedly quote discredited figures for the number of 'illegal aliens' said to be in South Africa and then very often go on to link those figures to the crime wave They are aided and abetted by some sections of the media who do not investigate but merely report inaccurate statements."[32]

As early as 1994, Home Affairs Minister Buthelezi depicted "illegal aliens" as a direct threat to the success of the Reconstruction and Development Programme (RDP), and to the safety and security of all South Africans.[33] In the same statement, Buthelezi drew direct links between migrants and crime, citing "evidence" that "aliens" were responsible for "criminal activities such as drug-trafficking, prostitution and money-laundering in what can only be described as typical Mafia-activity." He harshly condemned South Africans offering protection to undocumented migrants, and condemned citizens who employed "illegal aliens", announcing that he was "thinking of proposing to Cabinet consideration of legislation which will impose severe punishment for people who employ illegal aliens as it is in fact unpatriotic to employ illegal aliens at the expense of our own people." Further, Buthelezi encouraged citizens to become actively involved in the enforcement of the Aliens Control Act. He called on citizens to "aid the Department and the South African Police Services in the detection, prosecution and removal of illegal aliens from the country", emphasizing that the "cooperation of the community is required in the proper execution of the Department's functions."

In his 1997 Budget Speech to Parliament, Buthelezi said: "With an illegal population estimated at between 2.5 million and 5 million, it is obvious that the socio-economic resources of the country, which are under severe strain as it is, are further being burdened by the presence of illegal aliens."[34] In a Memorandum to Cabinet, Buthelezi called on his colleagues to declare "illegal immigration" the most important threat facing South Africa and proposed the adoption of "draconian" solutions to the "problem."

While Minister Buthelezi was the most vocal politician expounding on the threats of "illegal aliens", he was not isolated from the larger political climate in South Africa, which placed high value on restricting access, and controlling and limiting immigration.[35] Defence Minister Joe Modise publically blamed migrants for South Africa's spiralling crime rate: "As for crime, the army is helping the police get rid of crime and violence in the country. However, what can we do? We have one million illegal immigrants in our country who commit crimes."[36] In a speech made at a Defence Force Day Parade in 1997, President Nelson Mandela referred to the "threats posed by illegal immigrants, gun running and drug smuggling."[37] When Human Rights Watch produced a report critical of South Africa's treatment of foreign migrants, the organization was castigated by Buthelezi and the ANC Deputy Minister of Home Affairs. In 2000, a major "crime offensive" (known as Operation Crackdown) actually focused primarily on arresting and deporting irregular migrants. Police Commissioner Selebi and Minister of Safety and Security, Steve Tshwete, were unapologetic about evidence of police abuse of migrants.[38]

The idea that South Africa was being 'swamped' by Africa's poor and desperate was given regrettable "scientific legitimacy" by the Human Sciences Research Council (HSRC) which not only erroneously claimed that there were 5-8 million "illegal aliens" in the country but painted a picture of a country inundated by impoverished "floods" and "hordes" from the rest of Africa.[39] Conservative academics and an uncritical media perpetuated and intensified the hostile atmosphere.[40] In concert with the HSRC, the Home Affairs Department also succeeded in killing off the Southern African Development Community (SADC)'s Protocol on the Free Movement of Persons in Southern Africa in 1998.[41] Buthelezi responded to the Free Movement Protocol by stating: "South Africa is faced with another threat, and that is the SADC ideology of free movement of people, free trade and freedom to choose where you live or work. Free movement of persons spells disaster for our country."[42]

Meanwhile, Aliens Control Units were let loose on the streets and workplaces. Citizens planning anti-foreign attacks in May 2008 need have looked no further for inspiration than the often lawless activities of these Units in the 1990s as they swept through townships; arresting people at random on the basis of vaccination marks, skin colour or the way they pronounced words; tearing up documentation; allowing local residents to help themselves to the spoils; dumping the deportees in holding centres like the notorious Lindela and loading them up like convicts on trains at Johannesburg Station for the ride to Ressano Garcia on the border with Mozambique.[43] Many trains arrived virtually empty as the police accepted bribes to drop off people at stations in between so that they could return to Johannesburg. At a time when South Africa had no pro-active immigration policy (1994-2002), over 1 million people were rounded up under the 1991 Aliens Control Act and deported with no due process (over 90% to other SADC countries). Deportations have intensified still further since 2002 (Figure 1), exceeding 250,000 in 2006 alone.

Figure 1: Deportations of Foreign Nationals from South Africa, 1990-2006

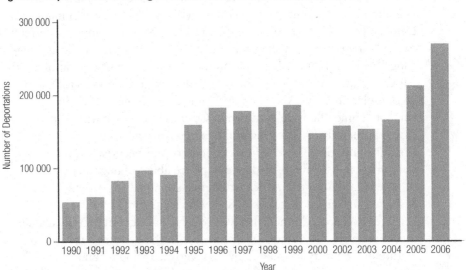

Source: Consortium for Refugees and Migrants in South Africa

Evidence of growing anti-foreign sentiment in the "new South Africa" after 1994 prompted SAMP (as one of its very first research activities) to examine the attitudes of South Africans towards migrants and immigration. In 1997, a national survey of South African attitudes on immigration was conducted and published.[44] The results shocked the researchers. First, as the study noted, opposition to immigration and foreign citizens was "widespread."[45] Second, South Africans were more hostile to immigration than citizens of any other country for which comparable data was available. Third, the public had actually become more intolerant since 1994. Another study, for example, showed that Mozambicans who had lived side-by-side with South Africans before 1994 were ostracized and marginalized after 1994.[46] Fourth, and most alarming of all, "these attitudes cut across income groups, age groups and groups with very different levels of education."[47]

There were some attitudinal differences by race but these were not large. In other words, SAMP concluded, unlike in other countries, it was impossible to identify a "typical" xenophobe. Xenophobia was too widespread and infected all sectors of society. SAMP had uncovered "an attitudinal profile that will not be easily overcome."[48] It urged government and the media to embark on a major public awareness and education campaign to counter xenophobia. Subsequent SAMP analyses of the South African media argued that the media was exacerbating rather than mitigating the spread and intensity of xenophobic sentiment.[49]

In the late 1990s, a number of local and international organisations released reports documenting intense anti-foreigner sentiment amongst South Africans, as well as rights abuses against migrants, asylum-seekers and refugees.[50] In 1998, in its Braamfontein Statement, the SAHRC noted that "xenophobia is a blight on our democratic values and should be eradicated."[51] COSATU's 2001 Statement on Xenophobia noted that xenophobia had grown to "unacceptable proportions" and called on government, civil society and all organs of the state to "prioritize the fighting of xenophobia."[52]

In 1999, SAMP repeated its attitudinal survey, adding an assessment of South African attitudes to refugees and refugee protection. Very little had changed, despite the best efforts of the South African Human Rights Commission and its "Roll Back Xenophobia" campaign. The survey confirmed "high levels of societal intolerance towards non-citizens (whether legal or illegal, immigrants or migrants, refugees or asylum seekers)."[53] Only 47% felt that South Africa should offer protection to refugees. As many as 70% felt that refugees in the country should never have the right to freedom of speech or movement. Less than 20% felt that refugees should always enjoy legal and police protection or access to basic services.

Once again, hostility to foreign migrants did not appear to be confined to any one racial, social or economic group. On many indices of xenophobia the South African population showed a 70:30 or 60:40 split but it was impossible to say with certainty which kinds of South African fell into each group. The study also found that while "white immigrants are not immune from the subtler forms of South African resentment their presence does not prompt the kind of panic and hostility that seems to attach to African migrants, immigrants and refugees."[54] Finally, the survey showed that South Africans' first-hand contact with other Africans in the country was relatively limited. As a result, "hostile attitudes are mainly driven not by experience but by stereotype and myth."[55]

A more sophisticated statistical analysis of the survey results examined how xenophobic attitudes were related to perceptions of deprivation.[56] It is well-known that unfavourable comparisons generate feelings of dissatisfaction, and these lead to prejudice and intergroup hostility, threats to identity and self-esteem, economic threat and frustration. This hypothesis was confirmed in the study. However, the study also examined how relative gratification affected attitudes towards non-nationals. Conventional wisdom is that the less people feel deprived, the less likely they are to display negative attitudes and behaviours. The study of South African attitudes found that "both relative gratification and relative deprivation are associated with greater levels of prejudice toward both African and Western immigrants to South Africa." In other words, in South Africa, those who perceive themselves as relatively more privileged display very similar prejudices to those who see themselves as relatively underprivileged.

In the years since 1999, a great deal of analysis has been conducted on the causes, consequences and impact of xenophobia by SAMP and others.[57] Government did not appear to heed the warnings of the SAHRC and COSATU and certainly did not move to root out xenophobia as both were demanding. Indeed, the SAHRC rolled up its Roll Back Xenophobia campaign in 2002 which surely cannot have been because they thought the problem was solved. Some effort was made by the Minister of Home Affairs to deal with xenophobia in her own department but the broader societal initiative called for in the 2002 Immigration Act did not occur.

When the AU's African Peer Review of South Africa criticized evidence of growing xenophobia in South Africa, the South African government took strong exception. The Peer Review Report had noted that "foreigners, mostly of African descent, are being subjected to brutality and detention."[58] Xenophobia was on the rise and should be "nipped in the bud." In its retort, the government nipped back at the Report: "the assertion that illegal immigrants are subject to brutal and inhuman treatment is strongly disputed."[59] Government said it did share the view of the Report that "much needs to be done to fight xenophobia" but did not say what it had done to combat a longstanding problem. The answer was very little. William Gumede, writing in The Independent, felt that "long-standing official denial of xenophobia is at the heart of the terrible violence" of May 2008.[60]

Violent attacks on non-South African migrants and refugees have also been a feature of the post-apartheid years (see Appendix). These attacks culminated in December 2005 in the disgrace at Olievenhoutbosch, a community near Centurion in Gauteng Province, when groups of South Africans chased foreign Africans living in the Choba informal settlement from their shacks, shops and businesses. Several people were killed in the burning and looting. The exact numbers killed, wounded, and dispossessed vary according to different sources. Throughout 2006 and 2007, attacks on foreign nationals escalated in their brazenness and brutality. In a spate of attacks in 2007, over 100 Somalis were killed and Somali businesses and properties were looted and torched. Certainly there were plenty of danger signs. Government ministers should not have been surprised by May 2008. The ingredients for the perfect xenophobic storm have been a decade or more in the making and many forecasters were predicting just such an outcome.

THE 2006 XENOPHOBIA SURVEY

SAMP's 2006 survey of South African attitudes towards migrants and refugees drew a nationally representative survey from respondents in all nine provinces of South Africa. Fieldwork was conducted in October and November 2006. In total 3,600 South African citizens over the age of 18 were randomly selected and interviewed. Survey respondents ranged in age from 18 to 97, with an average age of 38. Interviews with survey participants were conducted using a structured questionnaire. The content of the questionnaire was based on the research instrument originally used in the 1999 survey. However, several additional questions, primarily focused on self-perceptions were added to the 2006 questionnaire.

Further, a number of the five-point Likert scales used in the original questionnaire were adapted to nine-point scales, allowing for more nuanced and complex statistical analysis. The questionnaire was translated and administered in five South African languages: English, Afrikaans, Xhosa, Zulu and Tswana. Fieldworkers were fluent in the languages in which interviews were conducted, and survey participants were able to select one of the above as the preferred language for the interview. The final sample of 3,600 citizens consisted of 1,802 males and 1,798 females. The majority described themselves as black (70%), followed by white (13%), Coloured (12%) and Asian/Indian (4%) (Table 1).

Table 1: Respondent Profile by Race and Gender		
Race	Male (%)	Female (%)
White	14	12
Black	70	71
Coloured	12	13
Indian/Asian	4	4
N	1,802	1,798

As a subjective measure of income and poverty, respondents were asked to which "class" group they belonged. Within the total sample, 35% described themselves as "lower class" and 24% as "working class." An additional 31% of respondents viewed themselves as "middle class." Black (66%) and Coloured (62%) respondents were more likely to describe themselves as "lower" or "working class" than Asian/Indian (45%) or white (28%) respondents (Table 2).

Table 2: Respondent Profile by Race and Class				
Race	White (%)	Black (%)	Coloured (%)	Asian/Indian (%)
Lower class	3	46	19	9
Working class	25	20	43	36
Middle class	50	27	32	36
Upper middle class	15	3	3	6
Upper class	4	1	< 1	7
Don't know	4	4	3	6
N	462	2,527	442	141

Self-assessments of socio-economic class were generally consistent with household income, with 48% of respondents reporting a total household income of less than R3,000 per month, and an additional 16% less than R6,000. Reported household income differed significantly by race (Table 3). Overall, 24% of survey respondents were unemployed and looking for work at the time they were interviewed.

Table 3: Monthly Household Income by Race				
	White (%)	Black (%)	Coloured (%)	Asian/Indian (%)
Less than R3,000	7	59	41	17
R3,000 – R5,999	10	14	20	22
R6,000 – R8,999	12	6	10	11
R9,000 – R11,999	7	3	6	10
R12,000 – R15,999	9	2	3	9
R16,000 – R19,999	9	1	2	6
R20,000 or more	13	<1	1	6
No Answer	34	14	18	18
N	462	2,523	441	141

Most respondents had some formal education, with only 4% indicating that they had never been to school. About 14% had attended primary school, 37% secondary school, and 28% had completed Grade 12/Matric. An additional 11% had completed a diploma, although few held degrees (4%) or postgraduate diplomas (2%).

Respondents demonstrated high levels of civic and religious identity. More than 80% across all racial groups see being South African as "an important part" of how they view themselves, and a similar proportion want their children to "think of themselves as South African" (Table 4). Over 80% in all (and 92% of black respondents) agreed that they are "proud to be South African" though they were much less likely to agree that citizens of all races and religions share a common culture. However, the perception of diversity within South African society does not appear to diminish strength of civic or national identity.

Table 4: National identity*				
	White (%)	Black (%)	Coloured (%)	Asian/Indian (%)
Being South African is an important part of how I see myself	83	90	84	82
I want my children to think of themselves as South African	82	92	85	85
It makes me proud to be South African	84	92	84	84
In South Africa, it is clear that citizens of all races and religions share a common culture	39	50	51	46
*Percentage of respondents who "Strongly Agree" or "Agree"				

In terms of political affiliation, about 76% of the respondents said that there is a political party in South Africa that best represents their views. For a significant majority, this was the African National Congress (ANC) (61%), followed by the Democratic Alliance (DA)(8%) and the Inkatha Freedom Party (IFP)(2%). However, 18% said no particular party represented their views.

In terms of religious affiliation, the largest number indicated that they viewed themselves as Protestant Christians (56%), Catholics (11%) and Apostolic/Independent (11%). A further 77% indicated that they had "strong" or "very strong" religious beliefs, with 82% saying that it was important to them to be associated with their respective religion. Only 13% of the respondents said they were "not religious at all."

DO SOUTH AFRICANS WANT IMMIGRATION?

Both of SAMP's earlier surveys began with a general comparative question, developed by the World Values Survey concerning attitudes to the entry of foreign nationals into a country. SAMP now has data on this question for four time periods (Table 5). Compared to citizens of other countries worldwide, South Africans are the least open to outsiders and want the greatest restrictions on immigration (Table 6). The data indicates a hardening of attitudes between 1995 and 1999 with the proportion of people wanting strict limits or a total prohibition on immigration rising from 65% to 78% and the proportion of those favouring immigration if there were jobs available falling from 29% to 12%.

Two changes are evident since 1999. The proportion of people who are willing to consider employed-related immigration rose from 12% to 23% by 2006. In part, this reflects a policy shift by the government in 2002 which promoted a new skills-based immigration policy. At the same time, the proportion of those wanting a total ban on immigration increased from 25% in 1999 to 35% in 2006. Some 84% feel that South Africa is allowing "too many" foreign nationals into the country.

Table 5: South African Attitudes to Immigration				
	Let anyone in who wants to enter (%)	Let people come in as long as there are jobs available (%)	Place strict limits on the numbers of foreigners who can enter (%)	Prohibit people coming from other countries (%)
South Africa (2006)	2	23	38	37
South Africa (1999)	2	12	53	25
South Africa (1997)	6	17	45	25
South Africa (1995)	6	29	49	16

Table 6: Comparative Attitudes Towards Immigration				
	Let anyone in who wants to enter (%)	Let people come in as long as there are jobs available (%)	Place strict limits on the numbers of foreigners who can enter (%)	Prohibit people coming from other countries (%)
Nigeria (2000)	28	41	28	3
Peru (2001)	18	42	33	8
India (2001)	16	19	27	38
Philippines (2001)	14	18	58	10
China (2001)	14	48	27	11
Zimbabwe (2001)	12	53	26	9
USA (2001)	12	45	39	4
Argentina (2001)	11	45	34	10

Tanzania (2001)	9	20	66	6
Canada (2001)	7	49	40	3
UK (2001)	4	34	49	13
Egypt (2001)	4	43	40	13

Other findings included the following:

- In 1999, 66% of South Africans supported electrification of South Africa's borders. In 2006, this figure had risen to 76%, with only 2% strongly opposed.
- In 1999, 72% felt that foreign nationals should carry personal identification with them at all times. In 2006, this figure was still the same but only 4% strongly opposed the suggestion.
- There was a drop in support for penalizing employers who employ foreign nationals illegally (79% in1999 to 57% in 2006), perhaps because such sanctions rarely work and have not been implemented in South Africa.
- If migrants do come to the country, South Africans definitely think they should come alone. Less than 20% thought that it should be easier for families of migrants to come with them to South Africa.
- South Africans do not want it to be easier for foreign nationals to trade informally with South Africa (59% opposed), to start small businesses in South Africa (61% opposed), or to obtain South African citizenship (68% opposed).

Clearly dissatisfied with the volume and effectiveness of South African deportation policy (which has seen over 1.5 million people deported since 1994), the xenophobes on the streets have made it clear that they want all foreign nationals to "go home", even, it appears, those who regard South Africa as home. It is worth asking what South Africans, in general, feel about this form of "national cleansing" (Table 7):

- Nearly 50% support or strongly support the deportation of foreign nationals including those living legally in South Africa. Only 18% strongly oppose such a policy.
- Nearly three-quarters (74%) support a policy of deporting anyone who is not contributing economically to South Africa.
- The overwhelming majority (86%) support the deportation of those who have committed serious criminal offences.
- Two-thirds are not in favour of a policy that would give migrants without proper documentation the opportunity to legalize their status in the country
- And, perhaps most worrisome of all, 61% would support the deportation of foreign nationals who test positive for HIV or have AIDS with a mere 9% strongly opposed.

South Africans are divided on the issue of refugee protection with 47% supporting refugee protection and 30% opposed. Nearly 20% have no opinion on the matter. At the same time, nearly three quarters are opposed to increasing the number of refugees currently in the country and two-thirds are against offering permanent residence to refugees who have been in the country for more than 5 years. As many as half favour a policy of requiring all refugees to live in border camps. Only 6% are strongly opposed. Only 30% agree with allowing refugees to work and 60% want a policy of mandatory HIV testing of refugees.

Table 7: South African Attitudes to Enforcement Policies, 2006					
	Strongly Support	Support	Neutral	Oppose	Strongly Oppose
Deport All Foreign Nationals Including Those Living Legally in SA	17	30	14	22	18
Deport Those Not Contributing to SA Economy	42	32	9	10	3
Deport Those Who Have Committed Serious Criminal Offences	67	19	3	6	4
Legalize Status of Undocumented Migrants	10	16	8	19	46
Deport Those Who Are HIV Positive or Have AIDS	40	21	15	15	9
Give Asylum or Protection to Those Escaping War and Persecution	11	36	17	22	8
Grant Permanent Residence to Refugees in SA for Five Years	4	17	14	32	32

In sum, negative attitudes and accompanying support for harsh and punitive policy measures against foreign nationals are not confined to a fringe group in South Africa. They are widespread across the population. The majority of South Africans, still display all the hostility and intolerance that they did back in 1999. This leads us to the issue of rights for foreign nationals.

SHOULD FOREIGN NATIONALS HAVE RIGHTS?

In 1999, SAMP found that many South Africans were against extending the same basic rights to foreign nationals as to citizens (Table 8). In addition, South Africans distinguished between different categories of foreign national when they considered extending these rights. The rights in question were the right to legal and police protection, the right to access basic services and (in 2006) the right to access AIDS treatment. In 1999, less than 20% felt that refugees should always be entitled to these rights. In the case of "illegal immigrants" the figure was less than 10%. Temporary workers and visitors were viewed a little more sympathetically although only 13% felt they should automatically enjoy police protection.

In 1999, therefore, "illegal immigrants" were singled out for rights denial. This pattern was repeated in 2006. Since so many South Africans also believe that the majority of foreign nationals in their country are there illegally, this means, in effect, that they believe that basic rights should be denied to many if not most foreign nationals. With the exception of treatment for AIDS, at least two-thirds of South Africans still feel that irregular migrants in the country should be extended no rights or protection. Given that the police are believed to be major beneficiaries of the presence of irregular migrants (through bribery and protection rackets), it is alarming to see that so many South Africans feel that irregular migrants have sacrificed the right to police (and legal) protection by being in the country.

There have been some changes for the better since 1999. For example, there are drops in the proportion of South Africans who would deny basic rights to refugees and temporary workers and visitors, and a concomitant rise in those that do. The fact that the majority of South Africans still do not believe that any should automatically enjoy police or legal protection is still sobering, however. Again, while more South Africans now feel that refugees and temporary workers and visitors are entitled to access basic services, the majority are still opposed or feel that such access should be strictly conditional.

Answers to other questions in the survey were generally consistent with these findings. As many as 27% felt that a foreign national wanting South African citizenship should "abandon" their own language and culture. Only 15% totally disagreed with the proposition. Or again, almost half (49.2%) disgreed that new citizens should be allowed to use their own language and culture regardless of where they were. An astonishing 65% felt that all foreign nationals should be tested for HIV/AIDS and 56% felt that someone with HIV/AIDS should be precluded from citizenship. The idea that nationals from other countries pose a health threat to South Africans rather than the other way around seemingly will not die.

Table 8: South African Attitudes to Rights for Citizens, Migrants and Refugees						
	Always (%)		Sometimes (%)		Never (%)	
	1999	2006	1999	2006	1999	2006
Right to Legal Protection						
Citizens	91	94	9	5	1	0
Migrants/Visitors	13	33	43	38	44	29
Refugees	13	24	44	39	43	37
"Illegal Immigrants"	8	12	29	21	62	67
Right to Police Protection						
Citizens	93	94	7	5	1	1
Migrants/Visitors	24	48	53	36	23	17
Refugees	17	27	41	36	42	37
"Illegal Immigrants"	11	13	27	21	61	65
Right to Access Social Services (Education, Housing, Healthcare, Water)						
Citizens	96	96	4	3	0	1
Migrants/Visitors	30	49	46	32	25	19
Refugees	17	27	41	34	42	39
"Illegal Immigrants"	9	13	28	19	63	68
Right to AIDS Medications and Treatments						
Citizens		97		2		2
Migrants/Visitors		65		22		13
Refugees		50		24		27
"Illegal Immigrants"		38		19		43

DO SOUTH AFRICANS HATE OUTSIDERS?

While it is clear that South Africans favour highly restrictive, anti-immigrationist policies, it does not necessarily follow that they dislike foreign nationals per se (which would make them xenophobic as opposed to merely defensive and protectionist).

In South Africa, negative opinions on immigration go hand-in-hand with hostile attitudes towards foreign nationals. If xenophobes view foreign nationals as a threat, they will generally attribute negative motives to "the invader." In 1999, 48% of South Africans saw migrants from neighbouring countries as a "criminal threat", some 37% said they were a threat to jobs and the economy, and 29% that they brought disease. Only 24% said there was nothing to fear. In 2006, South Africans were asked why they think foreign nationals come to the country (Table 9). Looking for work (mentioned by 33%), conducting business (13%), and making money and seeking a better life (12%) were all mentioned. Those are, indeed, why most migrants come to the country.

South Africans are also alert to various push factors: poverty (mentioned by 10%), escaping war (6.7%) and food shortages and hunger. However, there is an undercurrent to all of this. For 21%, migrants come with the express purpose of criminal gain or to deal in drugs (7%). For 6%, foreign nationals come to "take jobs" and for 5% to destroy or corrupt "our country."

Table 9: Perceptions of Reasons Why Foreign Nationals Come to South Africa		
Reason	N	%
To look for work	1187	33.0
They come to commit crime	754	20.9
They come to do business	483	13.4
They come to have a better life	417	11.6
Running away from poverty	354	9.8
Other	307	8.5
They come to make money/They want to make money	278	7.7
They are here to deal in drugs	274	7.6
Come to escape war in their countries	240	6.7
They come to take our jobs from us	202	5.6
They are hungry/No food in their country	161	4.5
Our economy is strong	158	4.4
Don't know	140	3.9
They come here to study	94	2.6
To destroy our country	90	2.5
To corrupt our country	75	2.1
They are here for citizenship	54	1.5
They want to stay here	44	1.2
They come to earn a living	40	1.1
Totals	5352	
Note: respondents could give >1 answer		

South Africans continue to consider foreign nationals a threat to the social and economic well-being of their country. Indeed, along certain key measures attitudes have hardened since 1999 (Table 10). The proportion arguing that foreign nationals use up resources grew by 8% to 67% in 2006. The association of migrants with crime also intensified (45% to 67%) as did the idea that migrants bring disease (24% to 49%). The only positive sign was that more South Africans felt that foreign nationals bring needed skills to South Africa. At the same time, a third still believe that these skills are not needed.

Table 10: Perceived Impacts of Migrants		
% who agree	1999	2006
Use up resources	59	67
Take jobs	56	62
Commit crimes	45	67
Bring disease	24	49
Bring needed skills	58	64

Do South Africans dislike some "foreigners" more than others? As Table 11 shows, all foreign groups, wherever they are from, receive much lower favourability ratings than fellow South Africans. Of the foreign groups, people from Europe and North America receive the most favourable ratings from all South Africans. To say that they are particularly liked, however, would be incorrect. Just 22% of the respondents have a favourable opinion of foreigners from neighbouring countries, a percentage that drops to 16% for those from the rest of Africa. In both cases Asians provide the most favourable responses while Coloured respondents have the least favourable at just 15% and 11% respectively.

Table 11: Perceptions of Various Groups					
Favourable (%)	Whites	Blacks	Coloureds	Asians/ Indians	Total
South African Blacks	46	84	43	66	73
South African Whites	59	57	40	58	55
South African Coloureds	39	46	53	55	46
South African Asians/Indians	39	39	36	72	40
People living here from neighbouring countries	19	23	15	26	22
People living here from the rest of Africa	17	17	11	21	16
People living here from Europe or North America	26	21	19	30	22

To better understand where the unfavourable opinions of foreigners from African countries come from, and why the majority of xenophobic attacks are directed at Somalians, Zimbabweans and Mozambicans, respondents were asked to provide their opinion of foreigners from specific countries.

Migrants from Botswana, Lesotho and Swaziland are regarded in the most favourable light, although even here the majority of South Africans do not hold favourable opinions (Table 12). Thirty-nine percent, for example, hold a favourable view of Basotho (including 46% of black but only 17% of Coloured respondents). Swazi and Batswana received similarly favourable reviews from greater than one-third of respondents. Mozambicans (14%) and Zimbabweans (12%) are viewed in a much less favourable light by everyone. Most unpopular of all are Angolans, Somalis, Nigerians and Congolese.

Table 12: Perceptions of Foreign Residents by National Origin					
Favourable (%)	Whites	Blacks	Coloureds	Asians/Indians	Total
Nigerians	11	8	4	9	8
Angolans	14	9	5	7	9
Batswana	29	40	14	23	35
People from DRC	15	10	5	6	10
Ghanaians	16	12	4	9	11
Basotho	27	46	17	23	39
Mozambicans	13	15	9	11	14
Somalis	9	10	5	17	10
Swazi	24	44	18	32	38
Zimbabweans	12	13	9	11	12

DO SOUTH AFRICANS KNOW ANY FOREIGN NATIONALS?

One hypothesis about xenophobia is that "proximity to and social interaction with non-citizens will impact on citizen attitudes (negatively or positively)."[61] In SAMP's two surveys in the 1990s, respondents were asked how much contact they had with people from neighbouring countries in Southern Africa (from which the vast majority of migrants come). Surprisingly few was the answer (80% had little or no contact in 1997 and 60% in 1999) (Table 13). SAMP concluded that the vast majority of South Africans form their attitudes about other Africans in a vacuum, relying mainly on hearsay and media and other representations. Perceptions of, and attitudes towards foreigners were as a result of "second-hand (mis)information."

What is striking is that in 2006, the proportion with little or no contact has hardly changed. What has changed is the proportion with no contact at all which is down from 60% in 1997 to 32% in 2006. Those with a great deal of contact was only 4% in 1997 but had risen to 17% in 2006. In other words, while most people's attitudes are formed independent of personal interaction with migrants from neighbouring countries, more and more South Africans are interacting with non-nationals (and presumably having their prejudices confirmed by such interaction).

Table 13: Degree of Personal Contact with Migrants from Neighbouring Countries			
Amount of contact (%)	1997	1999	2006
A lot	4	8	17
Some	15	29	22
Little	20	16	29
None	60	44	32

The 2006 survey went one step further than its predecessors to see if the amount of contact differed by region of origin of foreign nationals. Here there were interesting differences. South Africans clearly have more contact with citizens of neighbouring countries than they do migrants from other regions. This is not surprising. However, they say they have an almost identical amount of contact with people from Europe/North America and the Rest of Africa. This is an important observation given the highly racialized nature of the xenophobic mania that has gripped the country. In general, though, nearly half of South Africans have no contact at all with people from these regions.

Table 14: Degree of Contact with Migrants from Different Regions, 1997-2006			
Amount of contact (%)	Europe/N. America	Neighbouring Countries	Rest of Africa
A lot	11	17	11
Some	17	22	17
Little	26	29	24
None	46	32	46

Does contact soften or harden attitudes? Asked how positive their interactions with people from other countries in Africa had been, one-third (34%) said the contact was positive, while 27% said it was negative. Asians gave, by far, the most positive responses. Almost half (47%) recorded positive experiences, while only 19% rated their interactions with foreigners as negative. Blacks were the most likely to say that their experiences were negative (29%) while Coloured respondents were the least likely to describe their experiences with foreigners as positive (24%). In other words, the experiences of the minority with contact were mixed. In some cases contact hardens, in others it softens. Contact therefore cannot be isolated from the circumstances of interaction.

DO FOREIGNERS STEAL JOBS FROM SOUTH AFRICANS?

There is a pervasive belief in South Africa that migrants are an economic burden and "steal" jobs from South Africans. The research literature suggests that these are stereotypes not grounded in reality. The "economic threat" posed by immigrants does not appear to be based on personal experience as most respondents have no personal experience of losing a job to a foreign national (85%) (Table 15). Around two-thirds say they also do not know anyone who has personally lost a job or heard of anyone in their community who has.

Table 15: Experience with Job Loss, 2006					
% Never	Whites	Blacks	Coloureds	Asians/ Indians	Total
Personally lost job to a foreigner	86	84	91	87	85
Personally know someone who lost job to a foreigner	73	67	73	78	69
Heard of someone in community who lost job to a foreigner	73	66	66	77	67

ARE ALL SOUTH AFRICANS EQUALLY XENOPHOBIC?

In the past, SAMP's instruments for measuring xenophobia did not allow for distinctions to be made between different groups in the population. In 1997 and 1999, as a result, there appeared to be very little difference between South Africans, irrespective of variables such as gender, race, income, and education. Our current approach sought to develop a general measure of xenophobia which would make it possible to differentiate between individuals and groups by assigning a "score" to each person surveyed. A scale was developed using combined responses from fifteen survey questions. Consistent with the responses used on the survey questionnaire, scores ranged from zero to ten, ranging from most to least xenophobic. Scores closest to zero indicate the most xenophobic attitudes, and scores closest to ten indicate the least. The scale was subjected to rigorous statistical testing to ensure validity, accuracy and strength.

On a scale of zero to ten, where 0 means "extremely xenophobic" and 10 means "not xenophobic at all" the average score was 3.95, suggesting that, in general, levels of xenophobia are high. Subtle differences in levels of xenophobia emerged between different groups in the sample. There were differences in the responses between race groups, for example. Coloured respondents had higher levels of xenophobia (3.57) than white (3.91), black (4.01), or Asian/Indian (4.13).

Respondents with Afrikaans as their home language displayed higher levels of xenophobia than all other language groups (3.57). Next were Xhosa-speakers (3.98), Sotho-speakers (4.01), Zulu-speakers (4.02), English-speakers (4.20) and Tsonga/Shangaan-speakers (4.20).

Subtle but significant differences also emerged in the average levels of xenophobia across respondents by class. Here we see a bimodal distribution with respondents who described themselves as "upper class" (3.72) as xenophobic as those from the "lower class" (3.72). Both are on average slightly more xenophobic than respondents in other class groups including "working class" (3.96) and "middle class" (4.12).

Consistent with this finding, there were differences between respondents in different income categories. Average xenophobia scores ranged from lows of 3.6 in the lowest monthly income categories of "R499 or less" and "R500-R899" to highs of 4.5 in the "R9,000 to R9,999" category and 4.8 in the "R16,000 to R17,999" category. This increase, however, did not appear to be entirely incremental, with mean scores dropping for example to 3.9 in the "R8,000 to R8,999" category and to 4.0 in the R18,000 – R19,999" category (Figure 2).

Figure 2: Level of Xenophobia by Income Group

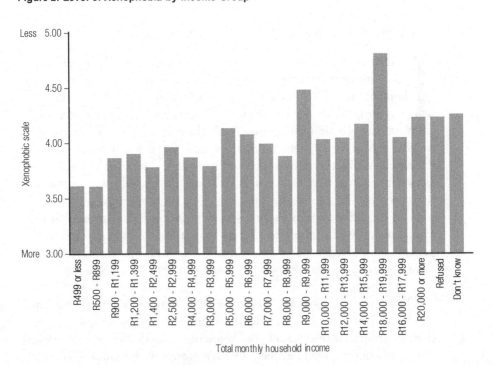

In general, this analysis suggests that xenophobic attitudes are stronger amongst whites than blacks and stronger amongst the poor and working class than the middle class. Education clearly has something to do with the latter finding. On average, xenophobic attitudes appear to be slightly more prevalent among those with less education. Xenophobia scores were greatest amongst the 127 respondents who had no formal schooling (3.43) and decreased in intensity with progressively higher levels of education (Table 16).

Table 16: Mean Xenophobia Score by Education		
Level	Score	N
No formal schooling	3.4	127
Primary school (up to grade 7)	3.8	498
Secondary school (grades 8 – 11)	3.9	1270
Matric/Grade 12	4.1	1010
Diploma after matric	4.0	369
Degree	4.3	129
Postgraduate diploma	4.0	52
Honours degree	4.4	32
Masters degree	4.3	13
Doctorate	5.0	8
Total	3.95	3508

Levels of xenophobia did appear to differ slightly by employment status. Respondents who were employed on either a full- or part-time basis scored an average of 4.1 and 4.0 respectively. Those who were unemployed and looking for work, and who could potentially be viewed as in closest competition with foreigners for jobs, scored an average of 3.85. The only differences of statistical significance were between those who were employed full time (4.10) and pensioners, who displayed the most xenophobic attitudes with an average score of 3.66.

Analysis of political party affiliation also showed slight differences. DA supporters have slightly higher levels of xenophobia with an average score of 3.6, compared to 3.96 for ANC supporters, 4.12 amongst those who support the IFP, and 4.02 amongst those who had no party preference.

On average, xenophobia scores vary slightly according to province, with highest levels in the Northern Cape (3.41) followed by the Eastern Cape and North West (both at 3.63), and the lowest in KwaZulu-Natal (4.22) and Limpopo (4.28) (Figure 3).

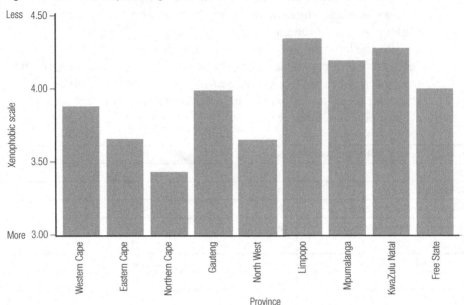

Figure 3: Level of Xenophobia by Province

WILL SOUTH AFRICANS ACT OUT THEIR PREJUDICES?

Interview a black African about living in South Africa and most will immediately tell you how hostile ordinary South Africans are to their presence. Every one has a story or knows of someone who has been verbally insulted or physically abused on the streets and in the communities of South Africa. Many have also had their businesses looted, property destroyed and their belongings stolen. Particular groups of African nationals, such as Somalis, have had it particularly bad. Recall 2007 and the nationwide attacks on Somali small traders and shopkeepers, many of whom have been given refugee status in the country by the government and are therefore here quite legally.

It does not seem to matter how long a foreign national has been in the country, whether or not they have legal documentation, whether or not they come from neighbouring countries with strong historical links with South Africa or whether or not they have married South Africans and have children born in the country. Many come from countries that suffered enormously as a result of their support of South Africa's liberation struggle. All are dubbed "amakwerekwere." All are outsiders. All are told they should "go home."

Xenophobic prejudice is sometimes subtle, sometimes blunt, sometimes violent, but always damaging and dehumanizing. Furthermore, black Africans will say that prejudice, name-calling and hostility is not confined to ordinary South Africans. Anyone with the misfortune to fall into the hands of the police speaks of the need to have bribe money at the ready to prevent summary arrest, the destruction of identity documents and the risk of being hauled off to Lindela and then home. When citizens attack foreigners, the police have often been accused of simply standing by.

In both 1999 and 2006, SAMP asked South Africans what, if anything, they would do about foreign nationals living in their communities. First, they were asked about the likelihood of their taking part in actions to prevent people from other Southern African countries from moving into their neighbourhood, operating a business in the area, being in the same classroom as their children or becoming a co-worker. What is striking is that almost a third of all respondents in both 1999 and 2006 answered that it was likely or very likely that they would take action to prevent these things happening. A disturbingly high proportion of the population in 2006 said they are likely to translate attitudes into action.

Table 17: Likelihood of Action Against Migrants from Other Southern African Countries			
Likelihood of Taking Action Action to Prevent Them (% Likely)	1997	1999	2006
Moving into your area	34	32	30
Operating a business in your area	34	32	32
Sharing a classroom with your children	31	27	26
Becoming a co-worker	32	27	26

A related question asked what sorts of actions they would take against foreign nationals. Most would confine themselves to "snitching" to the police (44%), community associations (36%) and employers (32%). A centrepiece of the 2002 Immigration Act, roundly criticized by human rights groups at the time, was "internal policing." Under these provisions of the Act, citizens were encouraged to report foreign nationals to the authorities if they suspected them of being in the country unofficially. For many critics, this seemed like a state license for social disintegration, suspicion, conflict and xenophobia. The 2006 Survey shows that citizens are all too willing to "do their part."

What is perhaps most significant, in light of later events, is that 16% of those interviewed said they were prepared to combine with others to force foreign nationals to leave their area and that 9% were prepared to use violence in the process (Table 18). Despite the widespread mayhem of May 2008, it is unlikely that 16% and 9% of South Africans were participants. What the SAMP survey indicates is that the violence could well have been even more widespread or may become so in the near future. At the very least, it suggests that a sizeable minority would have approved of the actions of others.

Table 18: Likelihood of Taking Action Against Foreign Nationals	
	2006
Report them to the police	44
Report them to my employer	32
Report them to local community association	36
Get people together to force them to leave	16
Use violence against them	9

CONCLUSIONS

> "We never mean for our prejudices to turn out violent but
> they do – often carried out on our behalves by this unwit-
> ting link: this quiet sharing of dirty thoughts by the one who
> means not to act it out and the other feeling there is legiti-
> macy in the maelstrom and so acts it out"
> (Saliem Fakir, 29 May 2008)

Stephanie Nolen of the Toronto Globe and Mail writes of a "sudden
eruption of xenophobic savagery" in South Africa.[62] Anyone who has
lived in South Africa since 1994, anyone with any familiarity with the
troubling history of post-apartheid xenophobia, will agree only that the
attacks were savage and ferocious. As for "sudden", SAMP and many
others have been warning for some considerable time that in the absence
of preventative action, such an outcome was almost inevitable.

Reflecting on the events of May 2008, President Mbeki recently
articulated what has now become the standard "official" explanation.
According to an article on the ANC Daily News Brief site, Mbeki
believes that the violence was driven "neither by antipathy nor a hatred
of foreigners." Apologising to all victims of the shameful actions, he
noted that they were purely the actions of "criminals in our midst" and
would be punished accordingly. He reportedly went on to assert that
those who claim the attacks were xenophobic were themselves guilty of
xenophobia: "No-one in our society has any right to encourage or incite
xenophobia by trying to explain naked criminal activity by cloaking it in
the garb of xenophobia."[63]

When SAMP embarked on its 2006 Survey of South African attitudes, it had hoped that the President was right in denying the existence
of xenophobia. Perhaps attitudes had changed since the xenophobic
heyday of the 1990s which had prompted the President himself to speak
out against xenophobia? However, instead of becoming more tolerant
and accepting of foreign migrants, the Survey showed that South African

attitudes have hardly changed at all. There are small glimmers of light (in changing attitudes towards rights for refugees for example). But when, in 2006, 76% of South Africans want their borders electrified, 65% want all refugees to be corralled in camps near the borders and 61% wish to expel any foreign national with HIV/AIDS, there is a deep and serious problem.

When Andile Mngxitama wrote in relation to the mayhem of May that "all South Africans are guilty" he spoke truth to power. Saliem Fakir, in similar vein, has identified the xenophobic "dirty thoughts" of fellow South Africans that license dirty actions.[64] This report has provided considerable evidence that such "dirty thoughts" are very real in the minds of many South Africans. Xenophobic attitudes are deeply-rooted, widespread and as entrenched as ever they were. Dirty thoughts can quickly lead to dirty actions, particularly given the fact that a sizeable minority of South Africans are primed for violent action against foreign nationals. They have done so with increasing venom in the last year, and they have done so with incalculable harm to the country in South Africa's recent "month of shame."

The xenophobic storm that has shaken the country to the core and besmirched South Africa's image around the globe has deep roots that stretch back to 1994 and well before. The savagery cannot be "blamed" on a small group of angry and disenfranchised poor people, angry with government and the ANC, and fed up with the growing numbers of desperate Zimbabweans in South Africa. We would argue that finger-pointing in this manner diverts attention away from a more fundamental issue: that South Africa has become and remains a deeply xenophobic society. Blessed with one of the most progressive constitutions in the world, accepted enthusiastically into the global community in 1994 and seen globally as an African leader, South Africa has shamed itself. And it has done so because xenophobia is not the preserve of an alienated few. It is widespread and pervasive, overt and subtle, permeating all interactions with non-South Africans and affecting the world-view and Africa-view of South Africans.

May 2008 need never have happened. But it is the culmination of a long process in which xenophobia was allowed, sometimes even encouraged, to grow unchecked. South Africa agonized about an immigration policy for eight years from 1994 to 2002 during which time xenophobia flourished, encouraged by reckless media reporting and a lack of political will.[65] When the SAHRC regrettably rolled up its Roll Back Xenophobia campaign in 2002, the voice of a strong independent critic of the treatment of foreign nationals in South Africa went silent. At that time, it appeared as if xenophobia was finally being acknowledged as a serious problem requiring urgent government intervention. President Mbeki had observed in 2001 that "we must be vigilant against any evidence of xeno-phobia against the African immigrants. It is fundamentally wrong and unacceptable that we should treat people who come to us as friends as though they are our enemies."

The 2002 Immigration Act (which replaced the profoundly xenopho-bic Aliens Control Act) also included the important provision that the Act should serve to ensure that "xenophobia is prevented and countered both within Government and civil society." In the 2004 Amendment Act, however, this requirement was changed simply to require that "xenophobia is prevented and countered." The Department of Home Affairs did establish a Counter-Xenophobia Unit through the mandate established in the Immigration Act, although serious questions exist as to how much this Unit has achieved. The upsurge in xenophobic violence is therefore a damning indictment of the general failure within South Africa to turn rhetoric into action, to effectively respond to or counteract xenophobia attitudes prevalent since 1994.

Even after 2002, there was no serious and systematic attempt to put in place government-wide mechanisms and programmes to give effect to the anti-xenophobia provisions of the new Act. Instead, the media con-tinued to rail against "floods of illegal aliens" and some police continued to treat foreign nationals as "mobile ATMs."[66] And the ANC govern-ment pursued SADC regional integration and pan-Africanism without ever convincingly selling either to its own electorate at home. Bold political leadership and a broad based public education campaign in the media, schools, communities and the work-place would have done much to mitigate and even avoid the mayhem. They could still.

Some ANC politicians have questioned how South Africans could attack black Africans from countries that had been so accommodating to South African exiles in the days of the anti-apartheid struggle. The key question is whether the exile experience has any resonance or meaning for the general populace. If everyone believed that South Africans should treat other Africans with tolerance and acceptance as pay-back for their past support, this should be reflected in positive attitudes towards the role played by those countries in the past and the way they treated exiled South Africans. Respondents in the Survey were therefore asked how well they thought South African exiles had been treated in other African countries. Nearly 20% of the respondents felt that the exiles had been treated badly. Another 41% had no opinion one way or the other. Only 39 percent agreed that they had been treated well or very well. In other words, it might be argued that nearly two out of three South Africans find the idea of reciprocity for past support of the liberation struggle either wrong or irrelevant. Further questioning would be necessary to prove this hypothesis.

POLICY RECOMMENDATIONS[67]

> "What's going to happen to us without barbarians? Those
> people were a kind of solution" (Constance Cavafy)

The tragic events of May 2008 should act as a major wake-up call to
all South Africans. They cannot rest on their laurels. Commissions of
investigation may or may not identify the causes of the mayhem. What
is urgently required is action, not only to ensure that the disgrace is not
repeated but that South Africans can hold up their heads as they prepare
to host a distinctly uneasy world in 2010.

All past and future perpetrators of xenophobic violence should be
vigorously prosecuted. There are signs that this is indeed what the state
intends though the penalties should be harsh and exacting for all of those
who broke the law, destroyed and stole property and engaged in rape and
murder. This is necessary not only to make an example of xenophobic
thuggery but to dissuade similar actions in the future. The citizenry needs
to know that despite its own dislike of foreigners, taking the law into its
own hands will not be tolerated. The state also needs to revisit past incidents of xenophobic violence and prosecute those involved as well.

While absolutely necessary, none of this is enough. Too many South
Africans, and too many police and officials, have engaged for far too
long in exploiting the vulnerability of foreign nationals. Corruption in all
aspects of the immigration system needs to become more costly than it
is worth to the perpetrators. At the same time, South African employers
who flaunt labour laws in their hiring and employment of migrants need
to be exposed and prosecuted.

The deeper problem of the widespread and entrenched xenophobic
attitudes identified in this report needs to be seriously addressed. There
is no reason why the majority of citizens should favour a particular
immigration policy provided they are well-informed about the purpose,
nature and impacts of that policy. But there is absolutely no reason, or
excuse, for that to be accompanied by abuse, hatred and hostility towards
migrants and "fellow" Africans in particular. We use that term advis-
edly since there is very little evidence that South Africans do view other
Africans as their "fellows" in any sense at all. How can attitudes that are
so entrenched, pervasive and negative be changed? In brief, by attacking
the disease of xenophobia with the same commitment that state and civil
society has shown towards attacking the scourge of racism in post-apartheid South Africa.

South Africa urgently needs an antidote to a decade of political inaction on xenophobia. Since 1994, South African attitudes have only hardened. What has been done is too little, much too late. Required now is
a broad, high-profile, multi-media, government-initiated and sponsored

anti-xenophobia education program that reaches into schools, workplaces, communities and the corridors of the public service. This programme should be systematic and ongoing. The programme needs to breed tolerance, celebration of diversity and the benefits of interaction with peoples from other countries.

As part of this effort, South Africans need to be educated about immigration and the benefits of managed migration. They need to know that immigration is not really as harmful as they think. They need to understand that immigration can be extremely beneficial. They need to know if it is. They need to be disabused of the myths and stereotypes they hold dear. They need to know what rights foreign nationals are entitled to when in South Africa. They need to be African and world leaders in refugee rights protection. They need to understand that South Africa is a member of a region and a world and has responsibilities to both. There needs to be informed public debate and discussion about pan-Africanism, the economic benefits of South Africa's interaction with Africa, and the need for immigrants. They need to abandon their myopic nationalistic siege mentality.

The events of May 2008 may provide the necessary spur to political action. Certainly the humanitarian response of many in civil society suggests that there are South Africans who are repulsed and ashamed by what their fellow citizens have done. Officials and politicians also need to move beyond rhetoric to action and example. Strong political leadership and will is required. South Africa cannot hold its head up in Africa, in SADC, at the African Union, or at any other international forum, if it continues to allow xenophobia to flourish. President Mbeki reacted with "disgust" to the events of May 2008. Disgust at xenophobic actions should translate into disgust at pre-existing and enabling xenophobic attitudes and a serious campaign to clear the minds of all citizens.

With the exception of the tabloid press, the media response to May 2008 has generally been exemplary in exposing xenophobia and fostering informed analysis and debate. It has not always been this way. The real tragedy of the last ten years is the way in which the media has mishandled the issue of xenophobia. Several research studies have shown how the media has uncritically reproduced xenophobic language and statements, time and time again. The media has certainly been complicit in encouraging xenophobic attitudes among the population. Journalists and editors at SAHRC-SAMP workshops on responsible reporting of migration issues in 2000-1 were extremely unresponsive to any suggestion that they played any role in encouraging xenophobic attitudes. Many remain so, protected by a misguided belief that all they are doing is reporting "the facts." They would not uncritically report the opinions of every racist they come across. No more should they uncritically tolerate the opinions of xenophobes.

A recent analysis of the UN Convention on the Rights of All Migrant Workers and Members of their Families shows that South Africa has not yet ratified the Convention.[68] The analysis shows that the treaty is not inconsistent with South Africa's human rights safeguards and labour law. However, there has been little public debate about the treaty and knowledge of its content and implications is appallingly low in official circles. South Africa should take the African lead in ratifying this convention and making the reasons clear to its own citizens. Commitment to, and adherence to, the Convention would help to clarify for all exactly what rights and entitlements foreign nationals have when in South Africa.

South Africa urgently needs an immigration policy overhaul. The fraught and protracted political process leading to a new Immigration Act in 2002 delivered a policy framework that is incoherent and, in many respects, unimplemented and unimplementable. Neither the post 2002 skills-based immigration policy associated with JIPSA nor the enforcement measures contemplated by the Act are working, precisely as SAMP and other critics predicted at the time. There is a need to develop a coherent and workable development-oriented immigration plan and to "sell" that plan to an electorate steeped in isolationism and hostility to immigration, despite the many demonstrable benefits it brings the country. No pro-active immigration plan can survive for long with a citizenry that is so uneducated about and sceptical of the benefits of immigration.

APPENDIX: XENOPHOBIA TIMELINE

1994

- The Inkatha Freedom Party (IFP) threatens to take "physical action" if the government fails to respond to the perceived crisis of undocumented migrants in South Africa.
- IFP leader and Minister of Home Affairs Mangosutho Buthelezi says in his first speech to parliament: "If we as South Africans are going to compete for scarce resources with millions of aliens who are pouring into South Africa, then we can bid goodbye to our Reconstruction and Development Programme."
- Violence erupts in a squatter camp in Hout Bay when Namibians are physically attacked by South African migrants who claim that the migrants are stealing "their jobs" in the fishing industry.
- Protestors in Alexandra Township march to the local police station with demands that include "Zimbabweans, Malawians and Mozambicans go home."
- Gangs of South Africans try to evict Mozambicans, Zimbabweans and Malawians from Alexandra township, blaming them for increased crime, sexual attacks and unemployment. The violent campaign, lasting several weeks, is known as "Buyelekhaya" (Go back home). One victim, Kenneth Ngwenya, had arrived in South Africa from Zimbabwe some thirty years previously.

1995

- A report by the Southern African Bishops' Conference concludes: "There is no doubt that there is a very high level of xenophobia in our country .... One of the main problems is that a variety of people have been lumped together under the title of 'illegal immigrants', and the whole situation of demonising immigrants is feeding the xenophobia phenomenon."
- A report by the HSRC, based on flawed methodology, claims there are 5-8 million "illegal aliens" in South Africa. The number is taken as fact by politicians and the media. The study is not withdrawn by the HSRC until 2001. The falsified numbers continue to be cited to this day.
- South Africa offers permanent residence to long-serving migrant miners from neighbouring countries. 51,000 miners from Mozambique, Lesotho, Botswana and Swaziland are granted permanent residence

1996

- Violent conflict between local and foreign migrants breaks out in Mizamoyethu, Cape Town. A one thousand strong crowd tries to drive foreign nationals out of the settlement. Two immigrants and two South Africans are killed. A peace accord is brokered by the ANC mayor, Dickie Meter.

- Local hawkers attack foreign traders in Germiston. One of the leaders of the foreign hawkers, Mr. Patrick Acho, is shot to death. Somali refugees are forced to stop hawking in Kempton Park after being threatened, and in some cases attacked, by local hawkers. On complaining to the police they are reportedly told "this is not your country, go back to your own country."
- At the urging of the Parliamentary Portfolio Committee on Home Affairs, Minister Buthelezi appoints an independent Green Paper Task Team chaired by Prof Wilmot James of Idasa.
- South Africa offers permanent residency to SADC nationals who have been living illegally in South Africa for more than five years. Over 200,000 apply and approximately 124,000 receive permanent residence.
- Residents of Alexandra demonstrate at the Department of Home Affairs in an attempt to disrupt the issuing of IDs to immigrants who they claim steal their jobs.

1997

- Defence Minister Joe Modise links the issue of undocumented migration to increased crime in a newspaper interview.
- In a speech to parliament, Home Affairs Minister Buthelezi claims "illegal aliens" cost South African taxpayers "billions of rands" each year.
- Local hawkers in central Johannesburg attack their foreign counterparts for two consecutive days, scattering and looting their belongings and beating the foreign traders with knobkerries. A flyer announcing the protest states "We want to clean the foreigners from our pavement." The chairperson of the Inner Johannesburg Hawkers Committee is quoted as saying: "We are prepared to push them out of the city, come what may. My group is not prepared to let our government inherit a garbage city because of these leeches."
- Five hundred South African hawkers march in Johannesburg chanting "chase the makwerekwere out," and "down with the foreigner, up with South Africans."
- A privatized deportation holding centre is established to process deportees. Called Lindela ("place of waiting"), the centre is initially operated by the Dyambu Trust, a venture set up by a group of top ANC Women's League figures
- A Southern African Migration Project (SAMP) survey of migrants in Lesotho, Mozambique and Zimbabwe shows that very

few wish to settle permanently in South Africa. A related study of migrant entrepreneurs in Johannesburg finds that they create an average of three jobs per business.

- A Draft Green Paper on International Migration is produced by an independent task team. It calls for a rights-based approach to immigration. Minister Buthelezi and his senior white officials are unhappy with the report and appoint separate task teams to draft refugee and immigration white papers under Departmental control.
- In December, the Cape Town Refugee Forum claims that 20 immigrants have been killed in the city as a result of xenophobia that year.

1998

- South Africa introduces its first refugee protection legislation. Problems of implementation bedevil the Act for many years leading to major backlogs of refugee claimants
- Three non-South Africans are killed on a train travelling between Pretoria and Johannesburg in what is described as a xenophobic attack.
- Two foreign nationals are "necklaced" (burnt alive) in Ivory Park, near Midrand
- In December The Roll Back Xenophobia Campaign is launched by a partnership of the South African Human Rights Commission (SAHRC), the National Consortium on Refugee Affairs and the United Nations High Commissioner for Refugees (UNHCR).
- The Department of Home Affairs reports that the majority of deportations are of Mozambicans (141,506) followed by Zimbabweans (28,548)
- A report by Human Rights Watch documents extensive abuse of migrants by employers and the police. The report is heavily criticized by the Deputy Minister of Home Affairs.
- Six white police set attack dogs on three Mozambican migrants and insult them with racist and xenophobic abuse. The incident is captured on video and aired to public outrage in 2000. The perpetrators are later tried, found guilty and imprisoned.
- SAHRC issues Braamfontein Statement on Xenophobia.

1999

- South Africa offers permanent residence to Mozambican refugees who have been in the country for 10-15 years. Approximately 90,000 applicants are successful. This brings the number of Mozambicans legally in South Africa to well over 200,000.
- A report by the SAHRC notes that xenophobia underpins police action against foreigners. People are apprehended for being "too

dark" or "walking like a black foreigner." Police also regularly destroy documents of black non-South Africans.

- SAMP releases a survey of South African attitudes to immigrants and immigration which shows that most South Africans share the same "stereotypical image of Southern Africans."
- The Department of Home Affairs releases a White Paper on International Migration and accompanying legislation calling for a new immigration policy. Human rights groups criticize both as a recipe for increased xenophobia. The new legislation stalls in Parliament and Cabinet for three years.
- Six foreign nationals accused of criminal activity are kidnapped by a mob in Ivory Park. Two are killed by "necklacing," three of the others are seriously injured and one manages to escape.
- Reports surface that undocumented Mozambican migrants being repatriated to Mozambique are regularly robbed, beaten and sometimes thrown from moving trains on the journey home.

2000

- Sudanese refugee James Diop is seriously injured after being thrown from a train in Pretoria by a group of armed men. Kenyan Roy Ndeti and his room mate are shot in their home. Both incidents are described as xenophobic attacks.
- In Operation Crackdown, a joint police and army anti-crime sweep, over 7,000 people are arrested on suspicion of being "illegal aliens." In contrast, only 14 people are arrested for serious crimes.
- A SAHRC report on the Lindela deportation centre lists a series of abuses at the facility, including assault and the systematic denial of basic rights. The report notes that 20 percent of detainees claimed South African citizenship or that they were in the country legally.
- A SAMP report on media attitudes to migrants finds evidence of xenophobic reporting by the press.
- Two Mozambican farm workers are assaulted at a farm by a group called Mapogo-a-Mathamaga after being accused of stealing by their employer. One of the men dies as a result of the attack.
- COSATU issues statement condemning xenophobia.

2001

- According to the 2001 census, out of South Africa's population of 45 million, just under one million foreign nationals are legally resident in the country. However, the Department of Home Affairs repeats its earlier discredited claims that there are more than seven million undocumented migrants.

47

- Three Somalis are attacked by a dog pursuing a burglar. When the policemen are asked to control their dog one responds with: "Don't tell me what to do you f----ing foreigners." Witnesses speak of the policemen claiming that they were checking to see if the dog could still bite.
- The chairperson of SAHRC accuses the Department of Home Affairs of being "rabidly xenophobic."
- SAMP releases a second report on South African attitudes to migrants. The report warns that xenophobic attitudes could turn violent.
- Wits academics, Klaaren and Ramji, release report highly critical of xenophobia and abuse of migrants by the police force
- SAMP argues that the number of undocumented migrants in South Africa is grossly exaggerated. The Head of Statistics South Africa, Mark Orkin, agrees and withdraws an earlier HSRC study.
- South African residents of the Zandspruit settlement near Johannesburg force hundreds of Zimbabwean residents from the area and burn dozens of homes after a Zimbabwean is accused of killing a local woman.
- Violent clashes break out in Milnerton between Angolans and South Africans who accuse the migrants of taking their jobs and women. Three Angolans and one South African, accused of killing one of the migrants, are killed.
- Writing in ANC Today, President Mbeki criticizes South Africans for their attitudes to other Africans.
- The SAHRC winds up its Roll Back Xenophobia Campaign due to lack of funding.

2002

- Parliament passes a new Immigration Act. As a result of criticisms of earlier drafts by human rights organizations, the Act promises to combat xenophobia but does not say how.
- A Nigerian man is beaten to death by three South African policemen.

2003

- A National Refugee Baseline Survey carried out by CASE finds that "Almost two thirds of applicants (63%) perceived South Africans in a negative light. In one third of the cases, applicants indicated that South Africans do not like foreigners, that they are xenophobic, and that they often refer to applicants as "makwerekwere" (a hate name for foreigners). In addition, 28% of applicants indicated that South Africans are particularly hostile and aggressive, often due to being ignorant about the plight of refugees."

- A survey carried out in Johannesburg and Hillsbrow finds that two thirds of respondents believe that foreigners are responsible for crime. 40 percent of foreigners surveyed have the same opinion.

2004

- Protests erupt at Lindela over claims of beatings and inmate deaths, coinciding with hearings into xenophobia by SAHRC and parliament's portfolio committee on foreign affairs.
- Violence breaks out between Xhosa and Shangaan speaking peoples in informal settlements near Rustenburg. Two are killed, four are injured and 52 families are displaced when their shacks are burned down.
- A fifteen year old South African boy is picked up by police who attempt to repatriate him to Mozambique, claiming that he is too dark to be South African.
- A Somali shop owner is shot dead in broad daylight in his own shop on Christmas Day. Nothing is stolen and xenophobia is thought to be the motive.

2005

- Three Somali refugees are stabbed to death outside their shop. The attacks are thought to be motivated by xenophobia and resentment of their successful businesses.
- A Human Rights Watch report documents the harassment, mistreatment and extortion of asylum-seekers and refugees by law enforcement agencies, the arrest, detention and threat of deportation of refugees and asylum-seekers as "illegal foreigners", and the unlawful detention and threats of deportation at Lindela Repatriation Centre.
- 146 people are arrested for malicious damage to property and theft following attacks on twelve foreign-owned businesses in Viljoenskroon.
- Zimbabwean and Somali refugees are beaten in Bothaville, in the Free State. The attacks occur after a community protest against the local municipality, and are accompanied by looting.

2006

- Somali shop owners in a township outside Knysna are chased out of the area and at least 30 spaza shops are damaged. Tensions start when an 18-year-old South African is shot by a Somali shopkeeper. After police arrest four robbery suspects and a shop owner, a crowd goes to all the Somali-owned shops in the area and destroys them.

- Violent riots erupt in Choba between foreigners and local residents, who claim that the migrants steal their jobs. Two are killed, including a Zimbabwean man who is burned to death.
- Two Zimbabweans are killed in violent clashes between South Africans and foreigners in the informal settlement of Olievenhoutbosch.
- Violence erupts against foreigners in Plettenburg Bay. Local residents claim that the migrants are stealing their jobs. At least one man is killed.
- Attacks occur against Somalis in the Cape Flats. During a period of just over a month, somewhere between 20 and 30 people are killed in townships surrounding Cape Town. Shops are robbed and looted. At least one Somali woman is shot, execution style, at a taxi rank.
- Somali-owned businesses in the informal settlement of Diepsloot, outside Johannesburg, are repeatedly torched.
- A gang vandalises more than 20 tuck-shops and fruit stalls owned by Mozambicans in Zamdela. 10 Mozambicans are injured when they are pelted with stones in the same attack.
- Somali refugees in Masiphumelele are attacked and shops looted and torched. Dozens are forced into hiding.
- The Baltimore Sun publishes an article called "Rising Tide of Xenophobia" about the particularly violent form of xenophobia that exists in South Africa.

2007

- UNHCR notes its concern over the increase in the number of xenophobic attacks on Somalis. The Somali community claims 400 people have been killed in the past decade.
- Anti-Somali riots are held in Port Elizabeth. Reuters reports that about 40 Somalis have been killed in Western Cape in a six month period.
- In Motherwell, over one-hundred Somali-owned shops are looted in a 24 hour period. A day later, more than four hundred Somalis leave the township in fear, most without any of their belongings.
- Mobs of youths destroy and loot shops belonging to Bangladeshi, Pakistani, Somali, and Ethiopian shop-owners in Ipelegeng near Schwiezer-Reneke.
- More than 20 people are arrested after shops belonging to Somalis and other foreign nationals are torched during anti-government protests in Khutsong township, southwest of Johannesburg.
- Shops owned and staffed by non-nationals are attacked and loot-

ed in Delmas. 40 non-nationals flee and are temporarily accommodated at mosques and with friends.
- A pub in Port Elizabeth bans Nigerians.
- Two Somali men are burnt alive in their shop in Mossel Bay the night after another Somali man is killed by armed gangs in Cape Town.

2008

January:
- Jeffrey's Bay: A crowd of residents attack Somali-owned shops and many Somali nationals seek shelter at the police station.
- Soshanguve: Four foreign nationals break into a spaza shop owned by a local trader. Residents apprehend the suspects and burn one to death. Residents call for foreigners to leave. Shacks are burnt and shops belonging to non-nationals looted. Many non-nationals flee the area.
- A community forum in Albert Park indicates that they want all foreign nationals living in the area to leave.

February:
- Itireleng: At a community meeting residents are encouraged to chase foreign nationals out of the area. Violent clashes take place. Shacks and shops are burnt and others looted.
- Valhalla Park: Residents forcefully evict at least five Somali shop owners from the area.

March
- Choba: 2 Zimbabweans are beaten to death by residents.
- Atteridgeville: At least 7 lives are lost in a series of attacks over a week. The deceased include Zimbabwean, Pakistani and Somali nationals as well as a South African who was mistaken for a foreign national. Approximately 150 shacks and shops are burnt down, destroyed or vandalized. Approximately 500 people seek refuge elsewhere.
- Diepsloot: 3 Zimbabweans are killed and shacks destroyed.
- Human rights organisations condemn a spate of xenophobic attacks around Pretoria that leave at least four people dead and hundreds homeless.
- Worcester: A large group of Zwelethemba informal settlement residents destroy foreign-run shops and leave a large number of foreign nationals homeless.

April
- Diepsloot: 30 shacks belonging to Zimbabweans are destroyed following a community meeting.

- Mamelodi: Fifteen shacks and spaza shops are burnt down. One girl is burnt to death in her shack.

11 May
- Alexandra: The most recent spate of xenophobic attacks begin when an angry mob takes to the streets in Alexandra Township, targeting foreigners who they say are not welcome in the country. Two are killed.

12 May
- Alexandra: A man is shot dead as violence continues.

13 May
- Alexandra: Foreigners take refuge at police stations and elsewhere to prevent further violent assaults on themselves and their property.

14 May
- Alexandra: Relative calm returns on Wednesday night following violence clashes between residents and the police. Heavy police presence in the township is maintained.
- Diepsloot: A mob throws stones at police and loots spaza shops. One man is injured.

15 May
- Cleveland: 5 people are killed and 50 injured in xenophobic attacks.

17 May
- Violence spreads to Thokoza and Tembisa.

18 May
- Alexandra: Another foreigner is shot.

19 May
- The death toll rises to 22 with many more injured and over 200 arrested.

20 May
- Boksburg: 1 person is killed and 2 critically injured in attacks.
- Johannesburg: 2 refugees taking refuge in a police station are seriously injured when they are stabbed on their way from the station to the shops.

21 May
- Violence spreads from Gauteng to Mpumalanga and KwaZulu-Natal. President Mbeki approves military involvement in the situation as the death toll climbs to 42.

23 May
- Violence spreads to Cape Town. Somalis and Zimbabweans are attacked by mobs and their shops vandalised and looted. Somali-owned shops are looted in Knysna.
- Mozambican officials claim that 10 000 of their nationals have left South Africa and returned home since the attacks began.

24 May
- Thousands of people take part in an anti-xenophobia march organised by churches and labour unions in Johannesburg
- President Mbeki is cricitised for his lack of action on the crisis.

25 May
- Mbeki condemns the attacks in a televised address, calling them an "absolute disgrace."
- Bakerton: Jacob Zuma speaks out against the attack in an address to thousands of people.

26 May
- Safety and Security Minister Charles Nqakula claims that the xenophobic attacks are under control. He adds that 1,384 arrests have been made.
- The death toll stands at 56 with 342 foreign-owned shops looted and 213 burned down. Tens of thousands more have been displaced

28 May
- The government denies having made a decision to establish refugee camps to house those displaced by the violence. A representative from the Department of Home Affairs admits that "temporary shelters" will be constructed.
- Police intervene when Somali nationals at a camp for displaced persons near Pretoria attack other foreigners trying to enter the camp.

2 June
- Hundreds of migrants, mostly Somalis, march to the South African parliament in a demonstration against xenophobia.

3 June
- Foreigners living in camps set up for those displaced by the violence call for the involvement of the United Nations because they claim that the South African government has failed them.
- Mbeki denies that the government was warned of the possibility of xenophobic attacks by the National Intelligence Agency over a year ago.

4 June
- The government expresses its commitment to reintegrating those affected by the xenophobic violence back into their communities.

5 June
- Senior prosecutors are appointed to oversee the prosecution of people arrested for involvement in the xenophobic attacks. Over 140 cases have been brought to court.

7 June
- Somalis in Port Elizabeth are attacked after the alleged shooting, by a Somali, of a local resident. Somali shop owners move their merchandise and police guard their shops.
- The Premier of the Eastern Cape and other local politicians gather to officially apologise to the foreign community for the xenophobic violence of recent weeks.

14 June
- Brazzaville: a Mozambican man is stoned and burned to death.

19 June
- An Ethiopian man is shot dead in Masiphumelele two days after returning home after the May attacks.

27 June
- Local residents in Ramaphosa warn that they are not happy about "foreigners" returning to their community.

3 July
- A Day of Remembrance is held as a tribute to the victims of May's xenophobic violence.
- President Mbeki notes that the violent attacks in May were not the result of xenophobia but rather of "naked criminal activity."

Compiled by Ashley Hill and Kate Lefko-Everett. Sources include: UN, Human Rights Watch, SAMP, SAHRC, Centre for the Study of Violence and Reconciliation, Wits Forced Migration Programme, Mail&Guardian Online, ANC News Brief, BBC News

ENDNOTES

1   "Minister: Xenophobic violence under control" *Mail & Guardian* 26 May 2008.
2   "Notes following briefing to media by Deputy Foreign Minister Aziz Pahad", 20 May 2008.
3   Ibid.
4   "Deputy President Phumzile Mlambo-Ngcuka speaks out against the violent attacks on foreigners and calls for calm" Statement issued by the Presidency, 23 May 2008.
5   William Gumede calls the government response "staggeringly unconvincing"; see "Mbeki must face up to South Africa's xenophobia" *The Independent* 21 May 2008.
6   "It was the Third Force in Alex" *Sowetan* 13 May 2008.
7   "Xenophobia attacks orchestrated by racists" *City Press* 22 May 2008.
8   "SA knew of xenophobia threat, says Kasrils" *Mail & Guardian Online* 24 May 2008; "SA caught off guard by xenophobic attacks: govt" *SABC News Online* 22 May 2008; "SA knew of xenophobia threat, says Kasrils" *Sunday Times Online* 24 May 2008.
9   "This is sowing hatred among Africans" *Sowetan* 23 May 2008.
10 "All of South Africa is guilty" *City Press* 17 May 2008.
11 Ibid.
12 "South Africa's long history of otherness" *Independent Online* 25 May 2008.
13 "Editorial: Days of our shame" *Mail & Guardian* 16 May 2008.
14 Ibid.
15 Adam Habib, "Explosion of a dream deferred" *The Star* 17 June 2008; E-K. Hassen and S. Gelb, "Today's protests are tomorrow's attacks" *The Star* 17 June 2008; M. Altman, "Desperation of SA's jobless youth major factor in violence" *The Star* 17 June 2008.
16 "Poverty a recipe for wider unrest" *IOL Online* 23 May 2008.
17 "A simple recipe for xenophobia" *Sunday Times Online* 19 May 2008.
18 "Msholozi has been warned" *Sunday Times Online* 28 May 2008.
19 Ibid.
20 "Days of our shame" *Mail & Guardian* 16 May 2008.
21 "Xenophobia: business in Africa set to take a dive" *Mail & Guardian* 31 May 2008.
22 "ANC's legacy of violence" *City Press* 31 May 2008.
23 "Mbeki's struggle for relevance" *Independent Online* 26 May 2008.
24 "South Africans take out rage on immigrants" *New York Times* 20 May 2008
25 "The shame of Thabo Mbeki" *Times Online* 20 May 2008.
26 "Xenophobic rage explodes in South Africa" *Globe and Mail* 20 May 2008.
27 "Xenophobia: Prince Buthelezi's prediction was ignored" Media Statement by IFP, 21 May 2008.

28 Human Sciences Research Council, *Citizenship, Violence and Xenophobia in South Africa* (Pretoria, 2008), p. 10.

29 "Pushed to the limit" *The Witness* 23 May 2008.

30 "We reacted quickly to attacks – Mbeki" *The Star* 27 June 2008.

31 J. Crush, "A Bad Neighbour Policy? Migrant Labour and the New South Africa" *Southern Africa Report* 12(1) (1996), p. 3.

32 S. Duncan, "Bad Law: Applying the Aliens Control Act" In J. Crush, ed., *Beyond Control: Immigration and Human Rights in a Democratic South Africa* (Cape Town, 1998), p. 151.

33 Budgetary Appropriation 1994: Review of Policy: Introductory Speech By Minister MG Buthelezi, Minister Of Home Affairs, 30 August 1994.

34 Minister of Home Affairs, Introductory Speech: Budget Debate, National Assembly, April 17, 1997; see also "Illegal immigrants cost SA taxpayer R2,75 billion a year" *Sapa* 4 January 1998.

35 See S. Croucher, "South Africa's Illegal Aliens: Constructing National Boundaries in a Post-Apartheid State" *Ethnic and Racial Studies* 21(1998); S. Peberdy, "Imagining Immigration: Inclusive Identities and Exclusive Immigration Policies in the 'New' South Africa" *Africa Today* 48(2001): 15-34.

36 "South African Defence Minister on arms sales" *London Al-Quds al-'Arabi* 19 November 1997, p. 6.

37 "Speech by President Nelson Mandela, at the Defence Force Day Parade" 26 April 1997.

38 'Selebi, Tswete say aliens not assaulted in swoop' *Sapa* 20 March 2000; 'No apology for arresting illegal immigrants: Tshwete' *Sapa* 28 March 2000.

39 J. Crush, "Making Up the Numbers: Measuring 'Illegal Immigration' to South Africa" SAMP Migration Policy Brief No. 3, Cape Town, 2001.

40 A. Minnaar and M. Hough, *Who Goes There? Perspectives on Clandestine Migration and Illegal Aliens in South Africa* (Pretoria: HSRC, 1996). On the media, see R. Danso and D.A. McDonald, *Writing Xenophobia: Immigration and the Press in Post-Apartheid South Africa*, SAMP Migration Policy Series No. 17, Cape Town, 2000.

41 See J. Oucho and J. Crush, "Contra Free Movement: South Africa and SADC Movement Protocols" *Africa Today* 48 (2001): 139-58.

42 "Keynote Address by MG Buthelezi, MP, Minister of Home Affairs" SAMP Conference on After Amnesty: The Future of Foreign Migrants in South Africa, Pretoria, 20 June 1997.

43 When the ATU's were disbanded, the SAPS took over the role of enforcers and did so with equal enthusiasm and disregard for the rule of law. For analyses of police abuse of migrants see J. Klaaren and J. Ramji, "Inside Illegality: Migration Policing in South Africa after Apartheid" *Africa Today* 48(2001): 35-48 and M. Madsen, "Living for Home: Policing Immorality Amongst Undocumented Migrants in Johannesburg" *African Studies* 63(2004): 173-92.

44 R. Mattes, D. Taylor, D. McDonald, A. Poore and W. Richmond, *Still Waiting*

for the Barbarians: SA Attitudes to Immigrants and Immigration, SAMP Migration Policy Series No. 14, Cape Town, 1999. The title of this study was based on the novel of similar name by J.M. Coetzee and referred to the xenophobic stereotyping of foreign nationals.

45   Ibid., p. 7.

46   M. Reitzes and S. Bam, "Citizenship, Immigration, and Identity in Winterveld, South Africa" In Crush and McDonald, eds., *Transnationalism and New African Immigration to South Africa*, pp. 80-100.

47   Mattes et al, *Still Waiting for the Barbarians*, p. 7.

48   Ibid., p. 26.

49   Danso and McDonald, *Writing Xenophobia*; S. Jacobs and D.A. McDonald, *Understanding Press Coverage of Cross-Border Migration in Southern Africa since 2000*, SAMP Migration Policy Series No. 37, Cape Town, 2005; see also J. Fine and W. Bird, *Shades of Prejudice: An Investigation into the South African Media's Coverage of Racial Violence and Xenophobia*. CSVR Race and Citizenship in Transition Series, Braamfontein, 2006.

50   For example, Human Rights Watch, *Prohibited Persons: Abuse of Undocumented Migrants, Asylum Seekers and Refugees in South Africa* (New York, 1998); SAHRC, *Illegal? Report on the Arrest and Detention of Persons in terms of the Aliens Control Act* (Johannesburg, 1999); B. Harris, *A Foreign Experience: Violence, Crime and Xenophobia During South Africa's Transition*. Violence and Transition Series, Vol. 5, Braamfontein, 2001; see also F. Nyamnjoh, *Insiders and Outsiders: Citizenship and Xenophobia in Contemporary Southern Africa* (London: Zed Books, 2006).

51   South African Human Rights Commission, "Braamfontein Statement on Xenophobia," 15 October 1998.

52   "Congress of South African Trade Unions (COSATU) Statement on Xenophobia" 8 February 2001.

53   J. Crush, *Immigration, Xenophobia and Human Rights in South Africa*, SAMP Migration Policy Series No. 22, Cape Town (co-published with SAHRC), 2001, p. 27.

54   Ibid., p. 28.

55   Ibid.

56   M. Dambrun, D. Taylor, D.A. McDonald, J. Crush and A. Meot, "The Relative Deprivation-Gratification Continuum and the Attitudes of South Africans Towards Immigrants" *Journal of Personality and Social Psychology* 91(6) (2006): 1032-44.

57   For example, Harris, *A Foreign Experience*; J. Mang'ana, 'The Effects of Migration on Human Rights Consciousness among Congolese Refugees in Johannesburg" MA thesis, Wits University, Johannesburg, 2004; J-P. Misago, "The Impact of Refugee–Host Community Interactions on Refugees' National and Ethnic Identities: The Case of Burundian Refugees in Johannesburg" MA thesis, Wits University, 2005; L. Landau, K. Ramjathan-Keogh and G. Singh,

"Xenophobia in South Africa and Problems Related to It" Forced Migration Working Paper Series 13, Wits University, 2005; F. Nyamnjoh, *Insiders and Outsiders: Citizenship and Xenophobia in Contemporary Southern Africa* (Dakar: Codesria Books and Zed Books, 2006); F. Belvedere, "Beyond Xenophobia: Contested Identities and the Politics of Refugees in Post-Apartheid South Africa" PhD thesis, University of Minnesota, 2006; J. Crush and W. Pendleton, "Mapping Hostilities: The Geography of Xenophobia in Southern Africa" *South African Geographical Journal* 89 (2007): 64-82; L. Landau and T. Monson, "Displacement, Estrangement and Sovereignty: Reconfiguring State Power in Urban South Africa" *Government and Opposition* 43(2008): 315-36.

58 African Peer Review Mechanism, *South Africa Country Review Report* No 5, September 2007, Paragraph 956.

59 Ibid., Appendix 2: Comments of the South African Government on the Report, Paragraphs 103-5.

60 "Mbeki must face up to South Africa's xenophobia" *The Independent* 21 May 2008.

61 Crush, *Immigration, Xenophobia and Human Rights in South Africa*, p. 5.

62 "Xenophobic rage explodes in South Africa" *Globe and Mail* 20 May 2008.

63 "Attacks on foreigners not xenophobic: Mbeki" *ANC Daily News Briefing* 3 July 2008.

64 S. Fakir, "It's about time our bubble burst" *South African Civil Society Information Service* 28 May 2008.

65 J. Crush and B. Dodson, "Another Lost Decade: The Failures of South Africa's Post-Apartheid Migration Policy" *TESG* 98 (2007): 706-9.

66 L. Landau, "Discrimination and Development? Migration, Urbanisation, and Sustainable Livelihoods in South Africa's Forbidden Cities" *Development Southern Africa* 24(2007), p. 69.

67 For other recommendations for corrective action see "Report of the Task Team of Members of Parliament Probing Violence and Attacks on Foreign Nationals" Cape Town, 26 May 2008; Consortium for Refugees and Migrants in South Africa (CoRMSA), *Protecting Refugees, Asylum Seekers and Immigrants in South Africa*, Johannesburg, 2008) and Vincent Williams, "Paranoid policy of migration control is not the answer" *The Star* 17 June 2008.

68 V. Williams, J. Crush and P. Nicholson, "The UN Convention on the Rights of Migrant Workers: The Ratification Non-Debate" SAMP Migration Policy Briefs No. 21, Cape Town, 2006.

MIGRATION POLICY SERIES

1. *Covert Operations: Clandestine Migration, Temporary Work and Immigration Policy in South Africa* (1997) ISBN 1-874864-51-9
2. *Riding the Tiger: Lesotho Miners and Permanent Residence in South Africa* (1997) ISBN 1-874864-52-7
3. *International Migration, Immigrant Entrepreneurs and South Africa's Small Enterprise Economy* (1997) ISBN 1-874864-62-4
4. *Silenced by Nation Building: African Immigrants and Language Policy in the New South Africa* (1998) ISBN 1-874864-64-0
5. *Left Out in the Cold? Housing and Immigration in the New South Africa* (1998) ISBN 1-874864-68-3
6. *Trading Places: Cross-Border Traders and the South African Informal Sector* (1998) ISBN 1-874864-71-3
7. *Challenging Xenophobia: Myth and Realities about Cross-Border Migration in Southern Africa* (1998) ISBN 1-874864-70-5
8. *Sons of Mozambique: Mozambican Miners and Post-Apartheid South Africa* (1998) ISBN 1-874864-78-0
9. *Women on the Move: Gender and Cross-Border Migration to South Africa* (1998) ISBN 1-874864-82-9.
10. *Namibians on South Africa: Attitudes Towards Cross-Border Migration and Immigration Policy* (1998) ISBN 1-874864-84-5.
11. *Building Skills: Cross-Border Migrants and the South African Construction Industry* (1999) ISBN 1-874864-84-5
12. *Immigration & Education: International Students at South African Universities and Technikons* (1999) ISBN 1-874864-89-6
13. *The Lives and Times of African Immigrants in Post-Apartheid South Africa* (1999) ISBN 1-874864-91-8
14. *Still Waiting for the Barbarians: South African Attitudes to Immigrants and Immigration* (1999) ISBN 1-874864-91-8
15. *Undermining Labour: Migrancy and Sub-contracting in the South African Gold Mining Industry* (1999) ISBN 1-874864-91-8
16. *Borderline Farming: Foreign Migrants in South African Commercial Agriculture* (2000) ISBN 1-874864-97-7
17. *Writing Xenophobia: Immigration and the Press in Post-Apartheid South Africa* (2000) ISBN 1-919798-01-3
18. *Losing Our Minds: Skills Migration and the South African Brain Drain* (2000) ISBN 1-919798-03-x
19. *Botswana: Migration Perspectives and Prospects* (2000) ISBN 1-919798-04-8
20. *The Brain Gain: Skilled Migrants and Immigration Policy in Post-Apartheid South Africa* (2000) ISBN 1-919798-14-5
21. *Cross-Border Raiding and Community Conflict in the Lesotho-South African Border Zone* (2001) ISBN 1-919798-16-1

22. *Immigration, Xenophobia and Human Rights in South Africa* (2001) ISBN 1-919798-30-7
23. *Gender and the Brain Drain from South Africa* (2001) ISBN 1-919798-35-8
24. *Spaces of Vulnerability: Migration and HIV/AIDS in South Africa* (2002) ISBN 1-919798-38-2
25. *Zimbabweans Who Move: Perspectives on International Migration in Zimbabwe* (2002) ISBN 1-919798-40-4
26. *The Border Within: The Future of the Lesotho-South African International Boundary* (2002) ISBN 1-919798-41-2
27. *Mobile Namibia: Migration Trends and Attitudes* (2002) ISBN 1-919798-44-7
28. *Changing Attitudes to Immigration and Refugee Policy in Botswana* (2003) ISBN 1-919798-47-1
29. *The New Brain Drain from Zimbabwe* (2003) ISBN 1-919798-48-X
30. *Regionalizing Xenophobia? Citizen Attitudes to Immigration and Refugee Policy in Southern Africa* (2004) ISBN 1-919798-53-6
31. *Migration, Sexuality and HIV/AIDS in Rural South Africa* (2004) ISBN 1-919798-63-3
32. *Swaziland Moves: Perceptions and Patterns of Modern Migration* (2004) ISBN 1-919798-67-6
33. *HIV/AIDS and Children's Migration in Southern Africa* (2004) ISBN 1-919798-70-6
34. *Medical Leave: The Exodus of Health Professionals from Zimbabwe* (2005) ISBN 1-919798-74-9
35. *Degrees of Uncertainty: Students and the Brain Drain in Southern Africa* (2005) ISBN 1-919798-84-6
36. *Restless Minds: South African Students and the Brain Drain* (2005) ISBN 1-919798-82-X
37. *Understanding Press Coverage of Cross-Border Migration in Southern Africa since 2000* (2005) ISBN 1-919798-91-9
38. *Northern Gateway: Cross-Border Migration Between Namibia and Angola* (2005) ISBN 1-919798-92-7
39. *Early Departures: The Emigration Potential of Zimbabwean Students* (2005) ISBN 1-919798-99-4
40. *Migration and Domestic Workers: Worlds of Work, Health and Mobility in Johannesburg* (2005) ISBN 1-920118-02-0
41. *The Quality of Migration Services Delivery in South Africa* (2005) ISBN 1-920118-03-9
42. *States of Vulnerability: The Future Brain Drain of Talent to South Africa* (2006) ISBN 1-920118-07-1
43. *Migration and Development in Mozambique: Poverty, Inequality and Survival* (2006) ISBN 1-920118-10-1
44. *Migration, Remittances and Development in Southern Africa* (2006) ISBN 1-920118-15-2

45. *Medical Recruiting: The Case of South African Health Care Professionals* (2007) ISBN 1-920118-47-0
46. *Voices From the Margins: Migrant Women's Experiences in Southern Africa* (2007) ISBN 1-920118-50-0
47. *The Haemorrhage of Health Professionals From South Africa: Medical Opinions* (2007) ISBN 978-1-920118-63-1
48. *The Quality of Immigration and Citizenship Services in Namibia* (2008) ISBN 978-1-920118-67-9
49. *Gender, Migration and Remittances in Southern Africa* (2008) ISBN 978-1-920118-70-9